IBM Personal Computer Program Writing Workbook

by George Bridges

ARCsoft Publishers

WOODSBORO, MARYLAND

FIRST EDITION
SECOND PRINTING

© 1983 by ARCsoft Publishers, P.O. Box 132, Woodsboro, MD 21798 USA

Printed in the United States of America

Reproduction or publication of the contents of this book, in any manner, without express permission of the publisher, is prohibited. No liability is assumed with respect to the use of the information herein.

Library of Congress (L.C.) Number: 83-5972

Trademark credits and software copyrights:
    IBM is a trademark of International Business Machines Corp.

    Programming advice and applications software in this book are copyright 1983 by ARCsoft Publishers.

    BASIC coding forms design and layout and graphics designing forms are copyright 1983 by ARCsoft Publishers.

ISBN 0-86668-818-8

IBM Table of Contents

The BASIC Programming Language 4

Computer Graphics 12

BASIC Coding Forms 14

Graphics Grids 94

Programming Books 96

The IBM BASIC Programming Language

IBM Personal Computer is practical, useful, fun, even exciting. But writing programs can be a drag unless you know BASIC, the most popular software language. In this book we will introduce you to the IBM P.C. BASIC in an easy-to-understand explanation of the most-used words.

In addition, we will provide you with 80 program-writing worksheets for your use in creating new and different software for your own IBM Personal Computer.

These worksheets are precision ruled so you can write as many program lines as you like and be able to keep them in a handy book for ready reference in the future.

We also provide several grids for your use in creating graphics designs for use on the IBM P.C.

IBM Personal Computer BASIC

Before writing programs for your IBM P.C. be sure you have thoroughly read and understand the owner's manual which came with your computer. It will tell you how to turn the machine on, how to hook up the accessories, how to type in new programs for the computer to run.

The introduction to IBM P.C. BASIC which we offer here will allow you to understand the most elementary workings of your computer and its program language. If you already know these basics, you can skip over our introduction and start using the coding-form worksheets immediately.

Notice that the worksheets have line numbers, in steps of ten, printed along the left-hand margin. The columns up to 80 are numbered across the top of the form.

The graphics grids are designed for your use in creating new and different video art on the TV monitor of your IBM Personal Computer. Visualize the squares on the grids as if they were the dots you can turn on and off on the face of your IBM P.C. TV picture tube. No matter whether you are working in low-resolution, medium-resolution or high-resolution graphics, these sheets will allow you to plan in advance your charts, graphs and other drawings.

This will be a straight-forward introduction to programming. We assume you have tried to read the owner's manual which came with your computer. You know how to turn it on. You know that pushing its buttons can't break it. Don't be afraid to experiment. We'll show you how to make it work for you.

However, the knowledge of BASIC which you will gain from this book will be applicable to *any* microcomputer, minicomputer, or main-frame computer using the BASIC language. And all of today's popular microcomputers use BASIC.

Our simple down-to-earth instruction will help you quickly understand how to talk to your computer and make it do what you want.

The name of the language is BASIC. That stands for *Beginner's All-purpose Symbolic Instruction Code.* What does that mean? Well, you know *beginner.* That's you. *All-purpose* means it's generally useful for lots of different things. *Symbolic* reflects the fact that the comuputer uses symbols to receive *instructions* from you. That is, symbols like the word PRINT or IF or THEN or FOR or NEXT. The symbols mostly are words you already know. *Code* is a buzz-word used by programmers to mean instructions to a computer.

So, you can translate *Beginner's All-purpose Symbolic Instruction Code* to mean "You use familiar words to tell your computer how to do just about anything."

BASIC was invented at Dartmouth College in the 1960s to be used by students, beginners, novices, newcomers, to computers and programming. It's very much like everyday English, as you'll see as we go through this book. We'll point out the familiar look-alike words which have meanings you already know and understand. Words like *end, for, go, to, if, then, list, new, next, step, print, return, run, stop,* and others.

Building on what you already know, we'll show you how the computer receives your instructions and uses them to do what you want.

Universal BASIC

We will use what we consider the most-universal form of BASIC, simplified so it is applicable to just about any contemporary computer—large or small. These words, when used to instruct a computer, would be understood by just about any hardware. Be sure to check your owners' manual to see how its BASIC words differ (if they do) from those we use here.

Keep your owners' manual handy as you type in and run programs. You may need it to make sure you are properly turning on your equipment.

Please remember, no two programmers write identical programs from scratch. Even when working toward the same goal, different writers will create different logic patterns. If your program doesn't exactly match a suggestion in this book, yours still may be correct.

Assuming your program runs and gets the required result, judgment of writing quality should be made on brevity, quickness of running time, and organizational clarity. It's always best to write as few lines as possible. The faster a computer completes its work, the better. And instructions should appear to flow in a logical order so they can be followed by others who might read your writing.

What's Inside Your Computer

There are four main areas : the *input* keyboard, the tiny *microprocessor,* a hulking *memory,* and the *output* display.

Processor, input, output and memory are the important parts of any computer. There are many accessory sections but those four are where the most- interesting activity occurs.

Input and output, often abbreviated as I/O, allow a computer to receive work orders from its operator, to receive information or data for use during a work period, and to send out messages and work results to the operator.

Through the keyboard, an operator gives the computer a list of instructions for carrying out one or more jobs. That list, or *program* of action, is followed by the computer whenever told to do so. It does not have to be acted upon immediately. The program can be remembered for later action.

To achieve some of its work goals, the computer must have additional information or *data.* That information also is typed in through the keyboard.

So, the keyboard has two functions: sending in programs of instructions and sending in additional data.

The output display might be a television set or a TV-like *monitor* or a larger electric typewriter. The output display has one main duty: showing messages and work results to you.

Memory

The convenience of a computer would be lost if we had to send in instructions, one at a time, and await action after each instruction. The beauty of the beast lies in its ability to memorize a long list of instructions and then, upon later command, execute those orders. The computer has a memory to store its various lists of instructions. It is called *program memory* and it can hold more than one complete program at a time.

At the same time, things would be slowed considerably if each extra piece of information has to be keyed in repeatedly every time the computer needed it. The computer can accept data one time and then store it away for repeated use later. To keep such extra information on hand, the computer has *data memory.*

5

Imagine 26 boxes labeled A through Z. The contents of the boxes can be changed. Some contain something. Some contain nothing. All are *variable* in that their contents can be changed.

Consider each box to be a single memory location, identified by its label A or B or C on through Z.

Strings

The boxes can contain either *numerical* information or words composed of combinations of letters, symbols and even numbers. Such a word is thought of as a *string* of data. Whenever one of our memory location boxes is storing a word, it is a *string variable.* If it holds only numbers, with no letters or other keyboard symbols, it is a *numerical variable.*

The quantity of letters, symbols and numbers which can be tied together in a string and stored in one memory location is limited. In larger desktop computers, one string in one memory location can hold hundreds of characters. But in some computers, one string is limited to seven characters.

This limitation applies only to string variables, not to numerical variables. Here are some examples of what variables contents might look like:

String Variables	Numerical Variables
JIM	86
@#$%ABC	1234567890
1/12/83	22.66
BIRTHDY	1

The program writer must keep track of which kind of variable is being used in a particular memory location. For example, if you store a word in location B and then try to use that data in a math problem, an *error* will occur and you'll get a message from your computer.

Only when you have numerical information stored in a memory location can you use that data for math.

One way programmers keep such things straight is by labeling string variables with a dollar sign ($). The dollar sign means *string* and should be read as "string."

Empty boxes

If we were to put a number in A we would label it A. If we were to put a word in A we would label it A$.

By the way, you can change the contents of the various boxes during the running of a program. A location can go from empty to full or from full to empty. Or a full location can have its value changed. A program can be written so the computer will continually check memory locations to see what has been stored there.

Obviously, when we say a memory location is empty we mean it has nothing in it. In effect, it has a big fat zero inside. As a matter of fact, if you were to look at the contents of an empty variable, you would see that it contains a zero. If you ask the computer to show you the contents of an empty memory location, the output display will show 0 if it is a numerical variable. If it is a string variable with nothing stored inside, the display will show nothing. Not even a zero. It will be blank.

You write in data memory by setting the data location letter equal to the value you want to write in it. For instance:

A = 1234

The value on the right is transferred into the storage location on the left.

Program memory

Now you know how to write information in data memory, and recall it. How about writing in program memory?

Your computer is built to use the BASIC program language. BASIC requires each line of a program to start with a *line number.* Here's a typical three-line program. Notice the numbers at the beginning of each line:

```
10  CLEAR
20  A$ = "WORD"
30  PRINT A$
```

The computer needs those line numbers to be able to follow your instructions in sequence. It knows that line 20 comes after line 10 and line 30 comes after line 20. Here's the same program with different line numbers:

```
  5  CLEAR
 21  A$ = "WORD"
189  PRINT A$
```

This program will run just the same as the first one. The line numbers are in the same sequence and the commands within each line are the same.

It is possible to write a program which uses every single step of program memory!

NEW

The command NEW erases everything stored in program memory, no matter how many different programs you have there.

The processor

Be an electronic mouse inside the computer again. Notice the master-controller in charge of everything. That's the microprocessor. *Micro* means small. *Processor* means it follows instructions in manipulating data to do work. It's not very big but it sure is powerful!

The processor is a very logical worker, dutifully going about its business in a proper order, carrying out instructions, doing work.

Built into the processor are instructions for how to handle its chores. As it follows that internal set of instructions, it knows how to follow your external set of instructions and do the work you want done.

To make a long story short, the processor takes information from memory, does something with it, and then either returns data to memory or displays it as output for you to read. It is able to do this many, many times each second and that's why we love the microprocessor!

Suppose you tell the microprocessor to fetch the contents of memory location B. It looks in there and finds WORD there. It *reads* that word, leaves the original behind in memory location B, and takes the information about what is in B away to work with it. The processor actually has a tiny memory inside itself so it can remember what it read in B.

If we instruct the processor to store something in memory location C, it *writes* data to that memory location. When it writes in that memory location, it destroys whatever was there before. For example, suppose we have the number 1234 stored in memory location C. As a result of an operation, we instruct the microprocessor to store the number 6789 in memory location C. It will put 6789 into C and we will lose the original number, 1234, forever.

Remember: reading destroys nothing but writing replaces old information with new.

In carrying out activities, the processor follows exactly the set of instructions you gave it as a *program*. It can't do anything else. If you make a mistake, it makes a mistake. If your work was perfect, its work will be perfect.

Program language

A program is composed of sets of alphabet letters which the processor understands as *words*. A complete set of such words makes up a *language*. BASIC is a language composed of words such as GO, TO, FOR, NEXT, IF, THEN, STEP, PRINT, RETURN, INPUT, PAUSE, WAIT, SET, STOP, END, SAVE, LOAD, GET, PUT, RUN, LIST, NEW and many others.

Since our computers are so very small, they have been given only the very best, most useful, of these words.

The more extensive the BASIC vocabulary, the more flexible the writer can be in creating programs. The total number of BASIC words invented to date is well over 500. You have the best of these in your computer.

It's easy to see why BASIC is the most popular computer language today. It's most like everyday English and, therefore, most readily used.

Writing and Running Programs

Writing programs means creating line lists of instructions and storing them, one at a time, in program memory.

Running means having the computer recall those sets of instructions, one line at a time, and do them.

RUN

Let's put an instruction in program memory and then run it.

RUN is an instruction to the computer to start at the lowest program line number and begin executing commands it finds there.

You can make the computer start its run at a different line number by typing that line number immediately after the word RUN. For instance, to start at line 100, type:

RUN 100

The computer will skip over any program lines with numbers less than 100.

REMarks

Suppose you were to write a very long, 50-line program of instructions for your computer. You might forget what each line was to accomplish. You need some way to put information in program memory which won't be acted upon by the computer during a run. Information such as notes to yourself so that when you list your program you can recall what the various parts of the program were supposed to do. These notes to yourself, and for other programmers to read, are called *remarks*. The REM command is used. Anything in a program line after REM will be ignored by the computer during a run. For example:

10   REM PRINT "NAME"
20   PRINT "WORD"

Type in this program and run it. You'll see that the computer has ignored, or skipped over line 10 and done line 20. Anything on a line after REM is ignored. Here's something different. Try this one:

10 PRINT "WORD": REM PRINT "NAME"

Here the program did the first part of line 10 but ignored the last half of the line following REM.

By the way, you put multiple statements in one program line by using the colon (:).

The colon indicates to the computer that a new statement is coming. Thus, you can place several statements in one line if you wish. Separate them with colons. Here's an example of a one-line program including several statements:

10 PRINT "WORD":PRINT "NAME": PRINT "DOG" :PRINT "CAT"

The computer will follow these statements of command in sequence as it reads through line 10. It will print WORD first, then NAME, then DOG, then CAT.

If, after typing in a program, you get an error message check your owners' manual to see how its BASIC words differ from those we use here.

REMarks are good for notes but very wasteful of memory. And we don't have much memory to spare in the computer. Use REM infrequently!

BREAK

What to do when your computer goes *blitzo!*
BREAK is used whenever you need to stop a RUN dead in its tracks. It's your panic button.

STOP

But suppose you want the program to STOP automatically at some point in a run? Use the STOP command. Write it into your program as one line.

How to continue after STOP? Use CONT. STOP stops it. CONT makes it continue.

END

You can, at your option, tell the computer a program has ended. Use the END command.
The CONT function won't work after an END command.

Input and Output

Input means giving the computer something to store in memory, whether data or program.
Output means displaying messages and work results for you to see.

INPUT

Information can be permanently placed in memory when you write a program. That is, data will actually be part of the program as written. This fixed information could look like this:

    10   A$ = "WORD"

Whenever you run the program the computer will always start with the memory that WORD is the data in memory location A$.

But, suppose you want the computer to pick up changeable data during a run? Use the INPUT function. Try this program:

    10   A$ = "IT IS"
    20   INPUT "WHAT IS THE WORD",B$
    30   PRINT A$;B$

When you run this program, the computer starts at line 10 and stores the string IT IS in memory location A. At line 20, the computer displays the question, WHAT IS THE WORD, and waits for a reply.   You type in any string of characters   in reply to give   your answer to   the computer.   The computer stores your   answer in B$. Then,   the   computer   moves   on   to   line   30 where it recalls the contents of memory locations A$ and B$ and prints them on the display.

Let's see how INPUT works when you want to collect numerical data. It works the same. Try this short program:

    10   Q = 111
    20   INPUT "PICK A NUMBER",N
    30   R = Q + N
    40   PRINT N;"PLUS ";Q;" = ";R

Here, line 10 puts the value 111 into memory location Q. Line 20 displays the message, PICK A NUMBER, and awaits your response. Whatever number you select, key it in. The computer will store your number in memory location N.

Line 30 does the math work for you by adding. It recalls that 111 was stored in Q and your number was stored in N. It adds those two values to get a new total. The total is stored in memory location R. The program moves on to line 40.

At line 40 the computer prints the results in sentence form. Try it with several different numbers. It's fun!

Suppose your number were 59. The program result, after printing line 40, would look like this:

    59   PLUS 111 = 170

You don't have to use the message part of the INPUT function if you don't want to. For instance:

    10   INPUT N
    20   INPUT P
    30   PRINT N
    40   PRINT P

This program allows the computer to take in your numerical data and store it in memory locations N and P and then print the values on the display. The computer will start at the lowest line number, as usual, line 10. Since no message has been supplied, the computer will display only a question mark (?). The ? tells you the computer wants some information. Try it on your computer.

PRINT

You already have used the PRINT output command but here's some further information.

PRINT causes a message to be displayed on the computer's display. The printed message consists of whatever is contained within the quotation marks following the PRINT command. For instance:

    10   PRINT "I LIKE ICE CREAM"

The computer reproduces exactly what you place between the quotes, including blank spaces. Try it in your computer. Now, type in this program:

    10   PRINT "I LIKE ICE CREAM"
    20   PRINT "DO YOU?"

These PRINT messages need not be in the same line as the PRINT command, by the way. Rather, you can store a message in data memory and recall it for PRINTing. For example:

```
10  N = 1234.56789
20  PRINT N
```

The computer, at line 10, stores the number 1234.56789 in memory location N. At line 20, the computer recalls the value of N and prints it on its display. Here's another example:

```
10  G$ = "WORD"
20  PRINT G$
```

Here the computer stores the string of characters, WORD, in memory location G. At line 20 it recalls G$ and prints it.

Here's an even more complex program:

```
10  A = 6
20  B = 7
30  C = 2
40  D = A + B + C
50  PRINT D
```

The computer stores the number 6 in memory location A; the number 7 in location B; and 2 in C. At line 40 it recalls the values in A, B and C and adds them together. The result of that addition is stored in D. Line 50 recalls the contents of D and prints the number on the display. Try it.

The Real Computer Power!

When folks talk about a computer having power, they often are referring to its ability to make decisions. And its looping ability. And its jumping ability. These capacities, when combined, make for some very powerful computing ability.

FOR/NEXT/STEP

You already know *loops* are fun but we need a way to control them to put them to a useful purpose. Here's one way:

```
10  FOR L = 1 TO 100
20  PRINT L
30  NEXT L
40  PRINT "END OF COUNT"
```

Lines 10 and 30 create a FOR/NEXT loop. A FOR/NEXT loop probably is the most frequently used of the super-power BASIC commands.

In this program, line 10 actually contains a built-in counter which advances the value stored in L by one every time the program reaches line 30. In fact, until the count reaches 100, line 30 causes the program to jump back to line 10. When the value in L reaches 100, then and only then will the FOR/NEXT loop let the action drop on down to line 40. Here's a variation:

```
10  FOR A = 10 TO 100
20  PRINT A
30  NEXT A
```

The memory location used in the loop can be any of those available to you in your computer.

Unless you tell it otherwise, the count will step up by ones. Try this change:

```
10  FOR X = 2 TO 40 STEP 2
20  PRINT X
30  NEXT X
```

Here the count goes up by twos. Try this program to make the computer count down by ones:

```
10  FOR J = 100 TO 1 STEP -1
20  PRINT J
30  NEXT J
```

The computer starts at 100 and counts down to 1, and then stops. Very convenient. Very powerful!

The STEP statement is not used unless you want increments other than +1. Minus numbers after STEP will cause the computer to count down in numbers while positive numbers will cause it to count up. Now make the computer take some giant steps:

```
10  FOR R = 999 TO 1 STEP -100
20  PRINT R
30  NEXT R
```

The computer counts down by hundreds. At that rate, it doesn't take very long to run out of numbers.

Sometimes you need a time delay in the middle of a program as it is running. The loop can be used to create such a time delay.

```
10  FOR N = 1 TO 999
20  NEXT N
```

Get a stopwatch and keep an eye on the running time for the program. Line 10 is a FOR/NEXT loop all on one line, without any output during the loop. The computer merely counts internally up to 999 and then moves on.

How long does it take such a loop to run its course? Use a stopwatch to time it. A nice long delay! Now try counting to 100:

```
10  FOR N = 1 TO 100
20  NEXT N
```

How long is the delay?

```
10  FOR N = 1 TO 10
20  NEXT N
```

Counting only to 10 reduces the delay.

```
10  FOR N = 1 TO 5
20  NEXT N
```

Counting only to 5 makes things happen even more quickly.

```
10  FOR N = 1 TO 3
20  NEXT N
```

Why is a one-second loop useful? Well, maybe you would like to turn your computer into a clock!

Here's a simple timer, for starts:

```
10  CLEAR
20  T = T + 1
30  FOR N = 1 TO 3
40  NEXT N
50  PRINT T ; " SECONDS"
60  GOTO 20
```

This is a crude clock. You can adjust its speed by changing the number 3 in line 30. It will count seconds until you stop it with the BREAK key.

Can you figure out why it takes a bit longer for the first display, 1 SECONDS, to appear? Because the computer uses up time as it works it way through lines 10, 20 and 30. You planned on it using up time at line 30 but you may have overlooked the amount of time it takes to carry out the instructions at line 10 and line 20.

IF/THEN

Did we say earlier the computer has the ability to make decisions? Yes! The IF/THEN statement is an important part of the decision-making process.

IF something happens or is true, THEN and only then will something else happen. IF nothing happens or something is not true, THEN nothing will happen. The IF/THEN test is one of the superpowers of the computer.

Here are examples of typical IF/THEN program lines:

```
IF A = 222 THEN PRINT A
IF B$ = "DOG" THEN 200
IF J = A/2 THEN PRINT J
IF Q$ = "WORD" THEN INPUT X$
IF T = 2*4 THEN 900
IF A$ PRINT B$
```

IF something is true, THEN some action is taken. That action can be a GOTO jump to a new program line. Or a PRINT command. Or an INPUT or any of the many BASIC statements.

Try this simple program in your computer:

```
10  A$ = "DOG"
20  B$ = "BONE"
30  IF A$ PRINT B$
```

The computer first stores string data DOG in memory location A and then BONE in B. Line 30 then causes the computer to examine location A and make a decision. The phrase IF A$ means "if there is anything in A$" then do whatever comes next in the same line.

In this case, we place DOG in A$ so we know the computer will find something there. Finding something there, it goes on to the last part of line 30 and carries out the specified action. It prints BONE on its display. If it would have found nothing there, it would have ignored the last half of line 30.

That was a simple test, merely to see if there happened to be anything in location A. Now let's change the program to make a harder test for the computer:

```
10  A$ = "DOG"
20  B$ = "BONE"
30  IF A$ = "BONE" PRINT A$
40  IF B$ = "BONE" PRINT B$
```

As before, line 10 stores DOG in memory location A$ and BONE in B$. Having done that, the computer moves on to do line 30.

At line 30, it finds an instruction from you to do a test and make a decision. The test is to look at the contents of A$ and see if they are BONE. If, and only if they are BONE, then go on to the last half of line 30. The last half of line 30 calls for the computer to recall the contents of A$ and print them on the display.

We know we stored DOG in A$. When the computer checks A$ it finds DOG, not BONE. Therefore, it uses its decision-making ability to proceed to line 40 rather than do the last half of line 30. It found that the IF A$ = "BONE" was not true so it could not go on to the last half of that line.

Since the line 30 test failed, the computer moved on to line 40. At line 40 it finds another test. It follows orders and checks the contents of B$. At B$ it finds BONE so the idea that B$ = "BONE" is true. With that found to be true, the computer decides to go ahead with the action called for in the last half of line 40. It recalls BONE from B$ and prints it on the display.

To recap, we stored DOG in A$ and BONE in B$. We asked the computer to print the word DOG if it found the word BONE in A$. It looked and did not find BONE so it did not print DOG. Then we asked it to print BONE if it found the word BONE in B$. It looked at B$, found BONE, and printed BONE on the display.

GOTO

You know that the computer does your list of BASIC instructions by following line numbers. First it does line 10, then line 20, etc. But, suppose you want the computer to do things in a different order. Maybe you would like it to *jump* over a group of lines. Or skip down to a different part of the program. This ability to *branch* out and around some lines to do other lines is an important power in the computer. It involves the GOTO and GOSUB statements.

GOTO means "go to a line." The GOTO statement must include the destination where you wish the program to go. For example:

GOTO 100

When the computer finds a GOTO statement, it immediately leaves the list, searches for and finds the destination line, and reenters operations at that point. Here's a small example:

```
10  GOTO 30
20  PRINT "NAME"
30  PRINT "WORD"
```

In this program, the computer starts at line 10 where it immediately finds a command to GOTO line 30. It skips down the list until it finds line 30. At line 30 it resumes doing what you asked. It prints WORD. In this case, the instruction in line 20 never gets done.

You can jump backward and forward within the program. Here's an example:

    10   INPUT "ENTER A NUMBER",A
    20   INPUT "ENTER ANOTHER NUMBER",B
    30   GOTO 100
    40   PRINT"THE TOTAL IS ";T
    50   GOTO 10
    100 T = A + B
    110 GOTO 40

Again the program starts running at the lowest line number, line 10. At line 10 it asks you for a number which it stores in memory location A. At line 20 it asks for another number which it puts in B.

At line 30 it finds an order to branch down to line 100 which it does. When it finds line 100 it does the instruction in line 100. It recalls the contents of A and B and adds them together, storing the total in T. Having completed line 100, it moves on down to line 110.

At line 110 the computer finds your instruction to jump back up to line 40. Doing that, it finds at line 40 an instruction to print THE TOTAL IS and the value in T. Putting that message on the display, it goes on to line 50.

At line 50 it comes upon your command to go up to line 10. It does that, thereby starting the entire process over again. The computer will go through this elaborate loop as long as you are willing to keep giving it numbers.

GOTO is, in fact, one of the most-used words in the BASIC language. Our programs are strewn with such jumps.

GOSUB/RETURN

Often you will need to repeat the exact same set of instructions at different points in a program. You could type the required program lines into the program each time they are needed. Or you can type them once and make the program jump to them when needed.

Typing of repeating sequences wastes your program-writing time, and, more importantly, wastes program memory space. It's easier for you and uses less memory when you create one *subroutine* to be repeatedly used by the computer.

Why not use a GOTO statement to get to a subroutine? The answer lies in the RETURN from the subroutine. If you were to use GOTO to get to a subroutine from several different places in a program, the designation of where to return to after completion of the subroutine would be long and clumsy. GOSUB was invented to take care of just that problem.

A subroutine is a small program which you can imagine as being set aside from the main program. A subroutine can be used as often as you like while running the main program. Each time a subroutine is completed, the computer automatically returns to the line in the main program immediately following the line from which it earlier had left the main program. Here's a small example:

    10   A = 555
    20   GOSUB 100
    30   PRINT T
    40   END
    100 T = A + 1
    110 RETURN

The main program is contained in lines 10, 20, 30 and 40. The subroutine is lines 100 and 110. The jump to the subroutine is the instruction in line 20. Note that it contains the destination line number. The return from the subroutine is from line 110 to line 30.

At line 10, we assign the value 555 to memory location A. At line 20, we ask the computer to branch to the subroutine at line 100.

At line 100 the computer finds an instruction to recall the value of A and add one to that value. The new total is stored in memory location T.

The program moves on to line 110 where it finds RETURN. That instruction, which must *always* be at the end of a subroutine, tells the program to jump back to the line immediately following the line where it left the main program. In this case, the program left the main routine at line 20 so RETURN will kick it back to line 30.

At line 30 the computer finds a command to recall the contents of T and to display it. It does that and moves on to line 40. At line 40 it finds the END command and ceases operations.

Why an END in line 40? Because you need to make sure the subroutine is entered only from the GOSUB instruction. After line 30, without an END in line 40, the program would automatically move from line 30 to the next available higher line number which is 100. At line 100 it would enter the subroutine. At line 110 it would find a RETURN which did not come from a GOSUB and an error message would occur.

Just as a GOSUB must have a RETURN, the RETURN statement must come after a GOSUB.

The computer has a tiny private "scratchpad" bit of memory within itself where it writes temporary notes to itself. When it executes a GOSUB command, it makes note of the line number from which it left the main program. Later, when it finds a RETURN, it refers to its scratchpad to see where it left the main program. It determines the next available program line after that exit point and re-enters the main body of the program at that point.

If the computer encounters a RETURN without having left the main program via GOSUB, it won't be able to find a "where to" note on its scratchpad and will send you an error message. You don't want error messages so you prevent the computer from getting into subroutines by means other than GOSUB jump commands.

11

Computer Graphics

Your personal computer is a system with four major parts: input, processor, memory and output.

Processor and *memory* are the innards, the brain which does the internal work you ask for.

Input is composed of the various parts of the equipment which allow you talk to the computer, to send in information for the memory to store and for the processor to work on. Input includes the typewriter-style keyboard, a tape, a disk, etc.

Output is the equipment available for the computer to talk back to you, to report the results of work you asked it to do. Output includes the video display screen, a line printer, or other devices.

This is concerned with a special use of one piece of output equipment, the video display screen. We hope you will learn from these pages how to make the computer display useful pictures on the face of the video tube.

When you turn the power on, the computer knows how to operate because the manufacturer has written software and inserted it into the computer's innards. That internal program is *system software*.

The computer can go beyond its basic internal housekeeping functions to do real-world jobs you ask of it because you write additional programs for it to follow. Your added instructions are *applications software*.

This, then, will show you how to write applications software especially to create pictures on the video display.

You hear a lot of talk, these days, about various types of *resolution*. Some graphics are said to be *low-resolution*. Some are *high-resolution*. There is a middle ground which could be thought of as *medium resolution*. What's the difference?

Low vs. high resolution

Letters, symbols, numbers, entire words, pictures, charts, graphs, anything displayed on the face of your TV screen or video display monitor is created as a series of lighted dots against a dark background. Imagine your TV screen as a large grid of tiny square rectangles like a piece of graph paper. Suppose you wanted to create the letter P on that grid, as in this approximate drawing:

The overall screen is dark. The light spots, when viewed together, create the image of the letter P. Your education leads you to see the letter P rather than an assortment of 13 white spots against a black background.

To create the letter P on the face of your TV, the computer lights several small rectangular dots in a pattern you recognize as P. The same for the letters C and A and T, the number 1 or the symbol we call an exclamation point or any others you can think of:

The size of the face of a TV set is fixed, but it is possible to make the lighted dots larger or smaller. The smaller the dot, the more dots we can squeeze onto the face of the video screen. Like creating graph paper with ever-smaller squares, the more dots we squeeze onto the face of the video tube, the less likely you are to be able to see any one dot.

Fewer dots filling a screen mean each dot is bigger, more easily seen. More dots filling a screen mean smaller dots, each less easily seen. For example, look at these two grids. Each is the same size. But one has twice as many small squares in it.

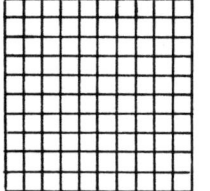 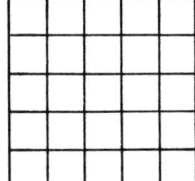

Let's try our letter P in each of two grids. The P on the left, below, contains more dots. We'll call it "high resolution" since it has a higher number of dots in the same space.

The P on the right contains fewer dots. We'll call it "low resolution" since it contains a lower number of dots in the same space:

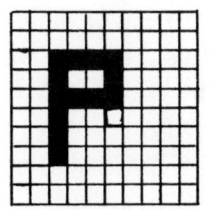 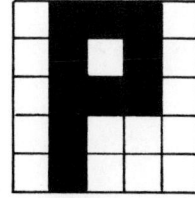

High Resolution   **Low Resolution**

If we had a P with more dots than in our low-resolution P, but with fewer dots than in our high-resolution P, we would have a medium-resolution P.

All information transmitted to you from the computer on the video screen is created the same way, as a pattern of lighted dots.

Text vs. graphics mode

Text mode is used for common letters, numbers, symbols, words, formulas and other kinds of frequently-used English-language communication. In the text mode, the computer calls upon data imbedded in its permanent memory to create the patterns of lighted dots we will recognize as letters of the alphabet or numbers or symbols.

The quantities and descriptions of those patterns of lighted dots are previously established inside the computer and beyond your control. Call for the letter A and you'll always get the same A. You cannot make that text-mode A short-legged or fatter or slimmer. In text mode, an A is an A is an A...

Graphics mode, on the other hand, is your own personal sketch pad. You can draw shapes and sizes of all sorts of characters and figures to suit your own desires.

When you turn power on, your computer wakes up in the text mode. Many of the BASIC words you use in programs automatically create text displays. For instance, use of the PRINT instruction makes a text display.

Video graph paper

Remember we said the TV screen can be imagined as having a grid like graph paper? Well, like graph paper you can precisely locate one spot on the face of the screen by counting rows and columns. Here's a grid:

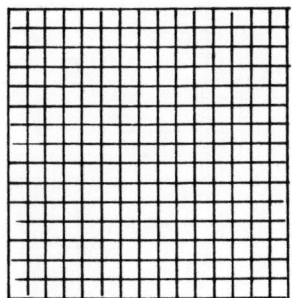

Now, suppose we thought of all the horizontal rows as X and the vertical columns as Y. We might think of lines moving across the TV screen as moving in the X direction and lines moving up and down the screen as moving in the Y direction.

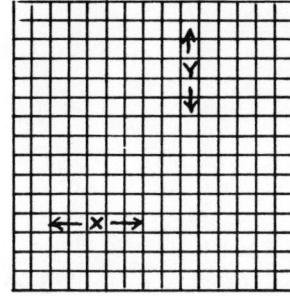

Count the dots across the grid. Start on the left and count toward the right. As you move toward the right hand side of the grid you get more and more dots. The number of dots is increasing. Each new dot adds one to the total. Each new dot is *plus* one.

Now move backward, right to left. Each new dot subtracts one from the total previously counted. Each is *minus* one.

To move left to right, then, add one to the value of X. To move right to left, subtract one from the value of X.

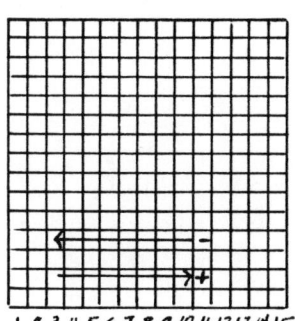

Similarly, to go up or down the screen, the value of Y changes.

Count the dots from bottom to top of the grid. Start at the bottom and count toward the top. As you move toward the top, you get more dots. The number of dots is increasing. Each new dot adds one to the total. Each new dot is *plus* one.

Now, move downward, from top to bottom. Each new dot subtracts one from the total previously counted. Each is *minus* one.

To move bottom to top, then, add one to the value of Y. To move from top to bottom, subtract one from the value of Y.

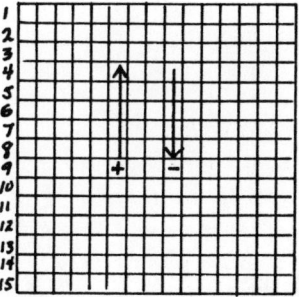

You will note that the position where X,Y is 1,1 is in the upper left hand corner of the grid in figures 8 and 9. What would the lower left hand corner be? Since it is in the fifteenth position for both X and Y it would be 15,15.

Any position on the screen can be located as an X,Y point. For instance 1,1 or 15,15 or 7,8. Where is 7,8?

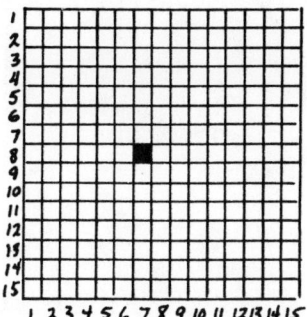

13

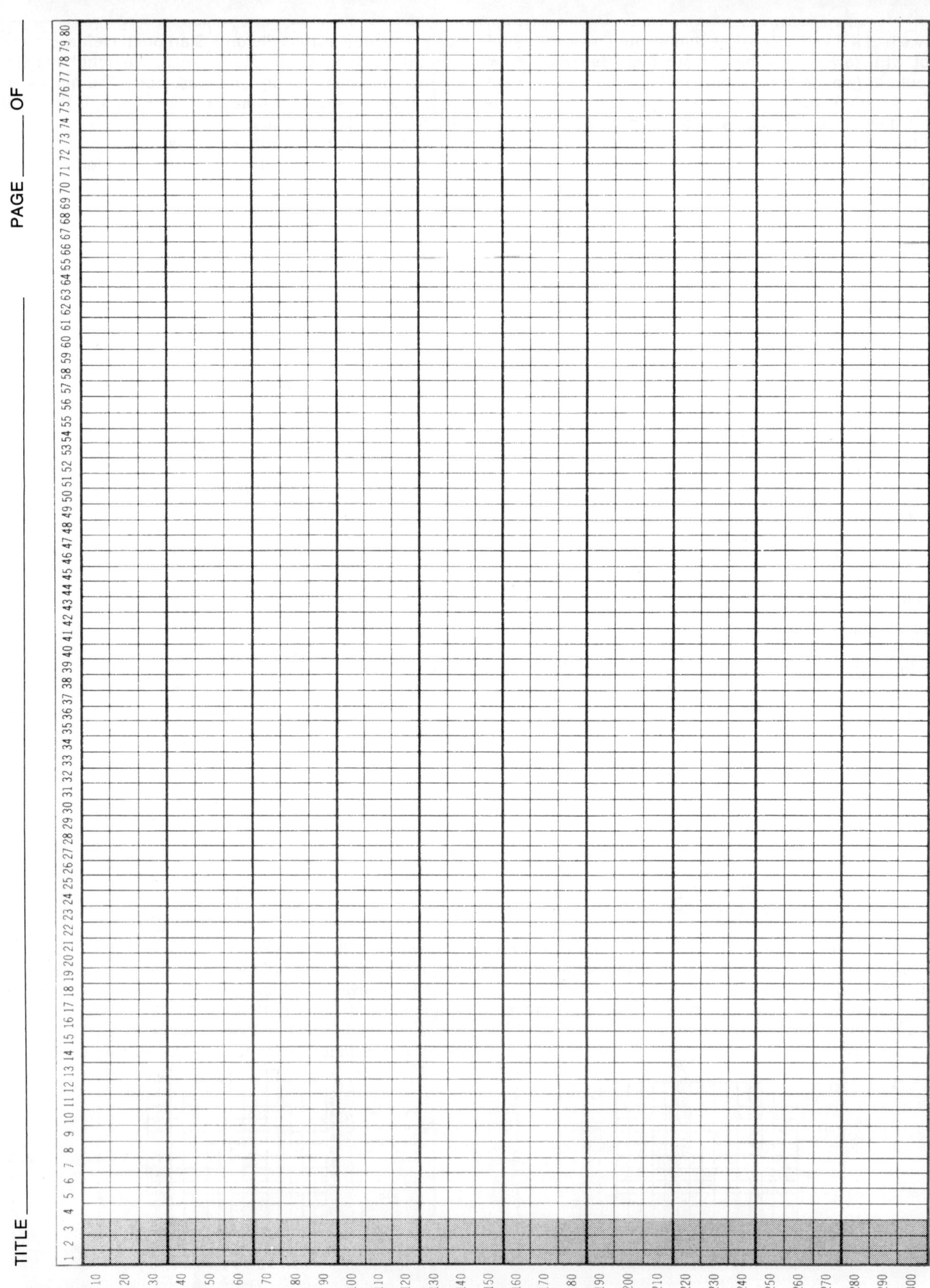

TITLE _____ PAGE ____ OF ____

TITLE _____ PAGE _____ OF _____

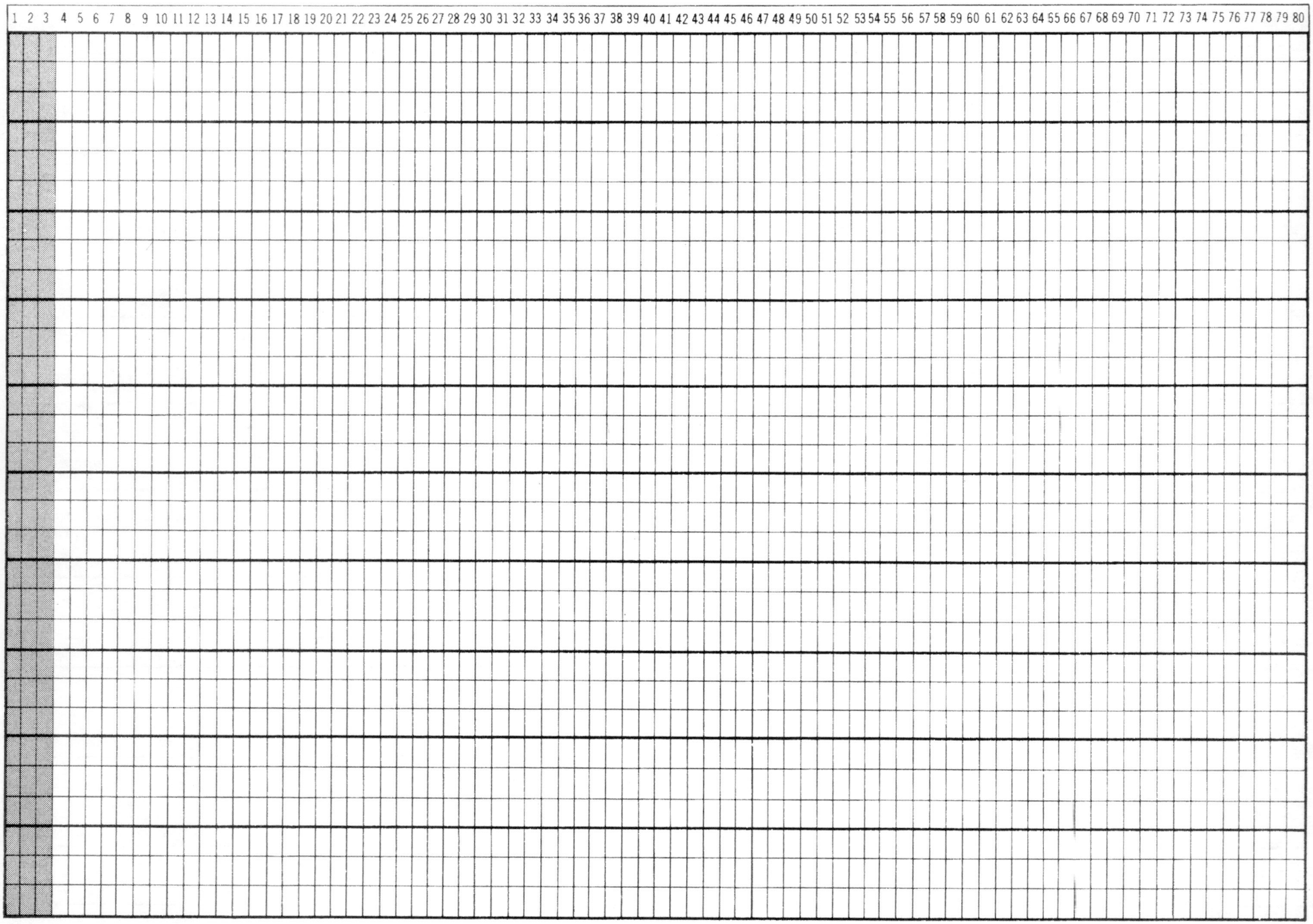

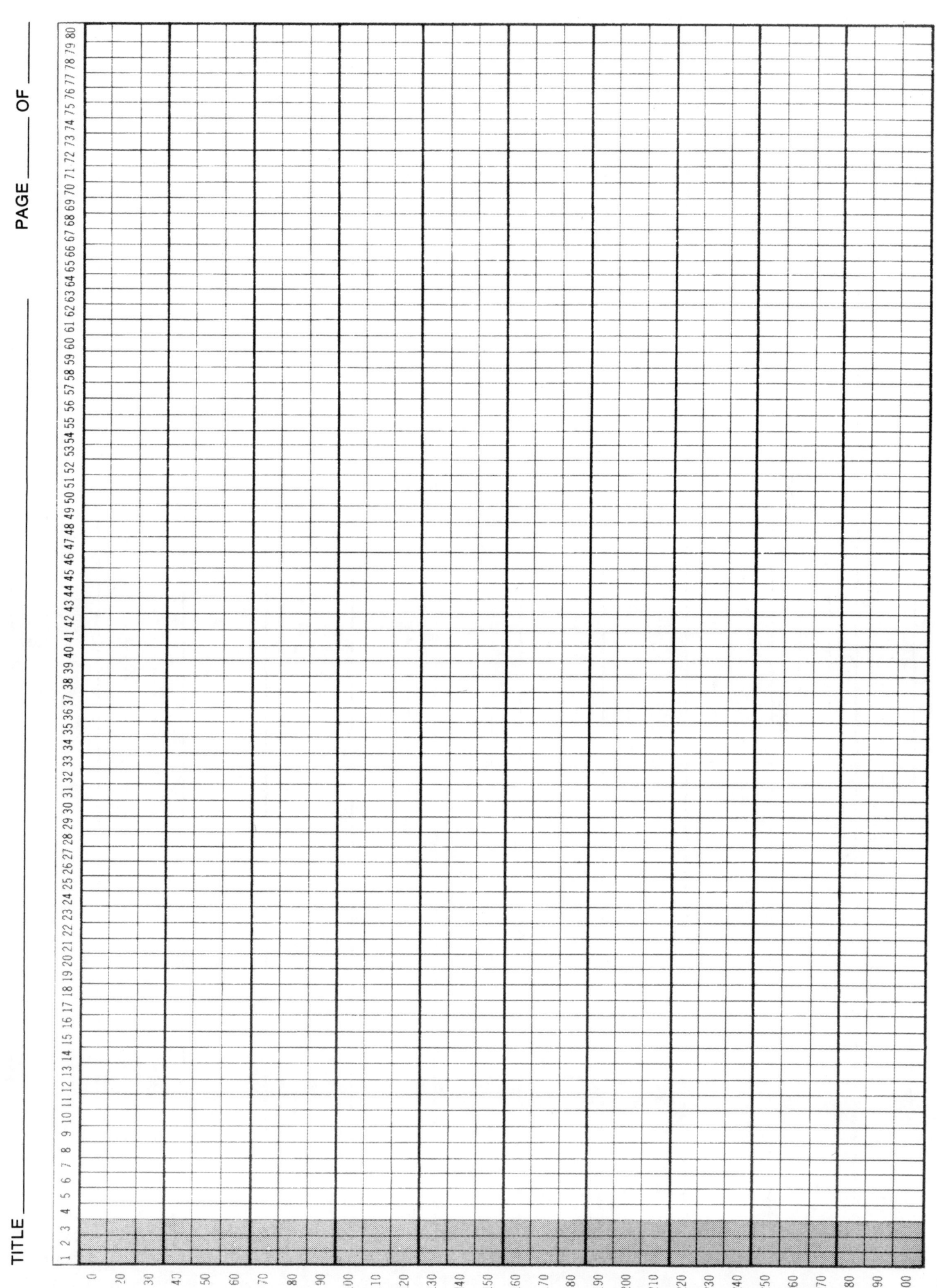

TITLE ______________________________ PAGE ______ OF ______

1 2 3 4 5 6 7 8 9 10 11 12 13 14 15 16 17 18 19 20 21 22 23 24 25 26 27 28 29 30 31 32 33 34 35 36 37 38 39 40 41 42 43 44 45 46 47 48 49 50 51 52 53 54 55 56 57 58 59 60 61 62 63 64 65 66 67 68 69 70 71 72 73 74 75 76 77 78 79 80

10
20
30
40
50
60
70
80
90
100
110
120
130
140
150
160
170
180
190
200
210
220
230
240
250
260
270
280
290
300

TITLE ______________________ PAGE ______ OF ______

1 2 3 4 5 6 7 8 9 10 11 12 13 14 15 16 17 18 19 20 21 22 23 24 25 26 27 28 29 30 31 32 33 34 35 36 37 38 39 40 41 42 43 44 45 46 47 48 49 50 51 52 53 54 55 56 57 58 59 60 61 62 63 64 65 66 67 68 69 70 71 72 73 74 75 76 77 78 79 80

10
20
30
40
50
60
70
80
90
100
110
120
130
140
150
160
170
180
190
200
210
220
230
240
250
260
270
280
290
300

TITLE ______________________________ PAGE ______ OF ______

	1	2	3	4	5	6	7	8	9	10	11	12	13	14	15	16	17	18	19	20	21	22	23	24	25	26	27	28	29	30	31	32	33	34	35	36	37	38	39	40	41	42	43	44	45	46	47	48	49	50	51	52	53	54	55	56	57	58	59	60	61	62	63	64	65	66	67	68	69	70	71	72	73	74	75	76	77	78	79	80
10																																																																																
20																																																																																
30																																																																																
40																																																																																
50																																																																																
60																																																																																
70																																																																																
80																																																																																
90																																																																																
100																																																																																
110																																																																																
120																																																																																
130																																																																																
140																																																																																
150																																																																																
160																																																																																
170																																																																																
180																																																																																
190																																																																																
200																																																																																
210																																																																																
220																																																																																
230																																																																																
240																																																																																
250																																																																																
260																																																																																
270																																																																																
280																																																																																
290																																																																																
300																																																																																

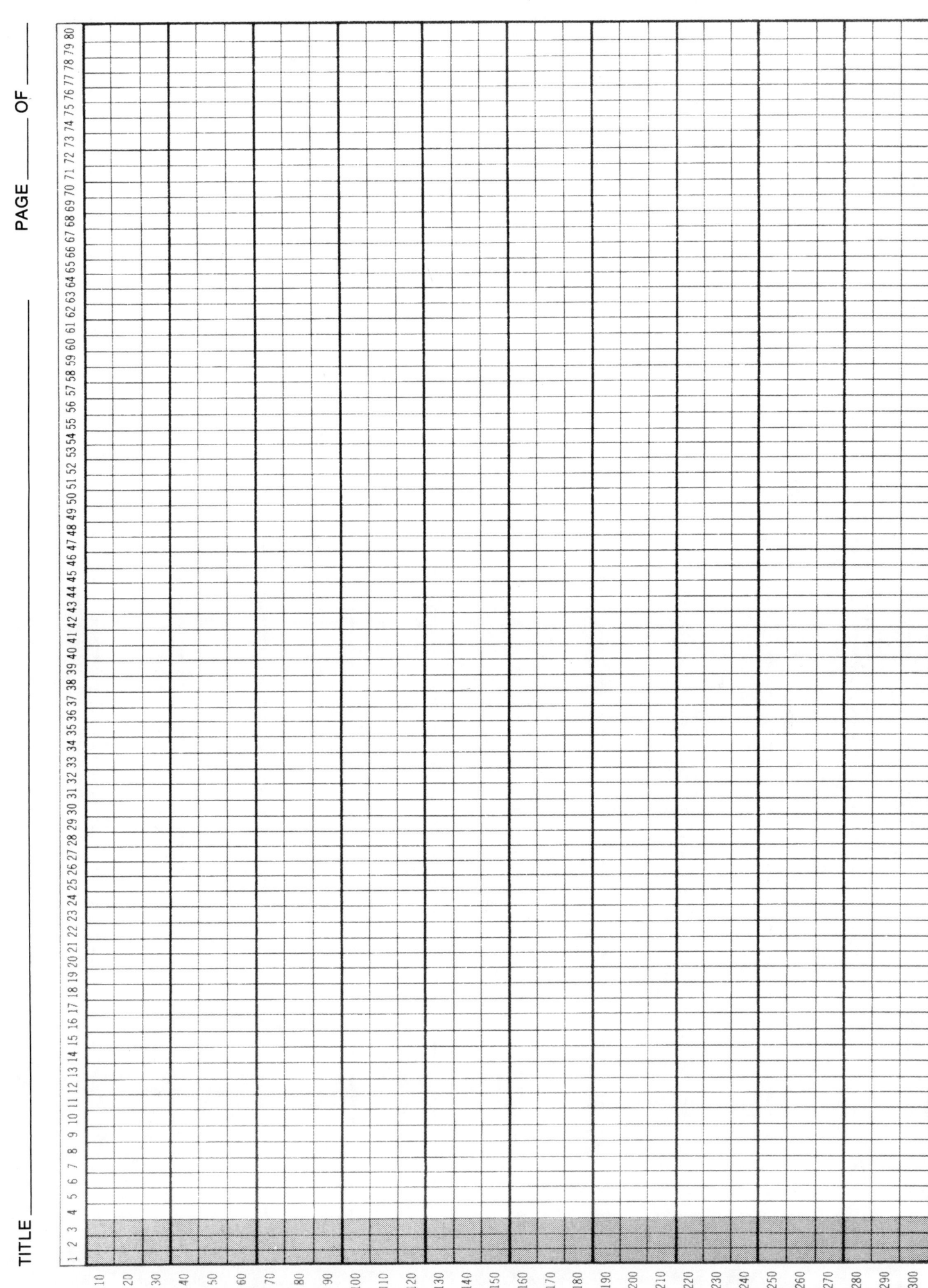

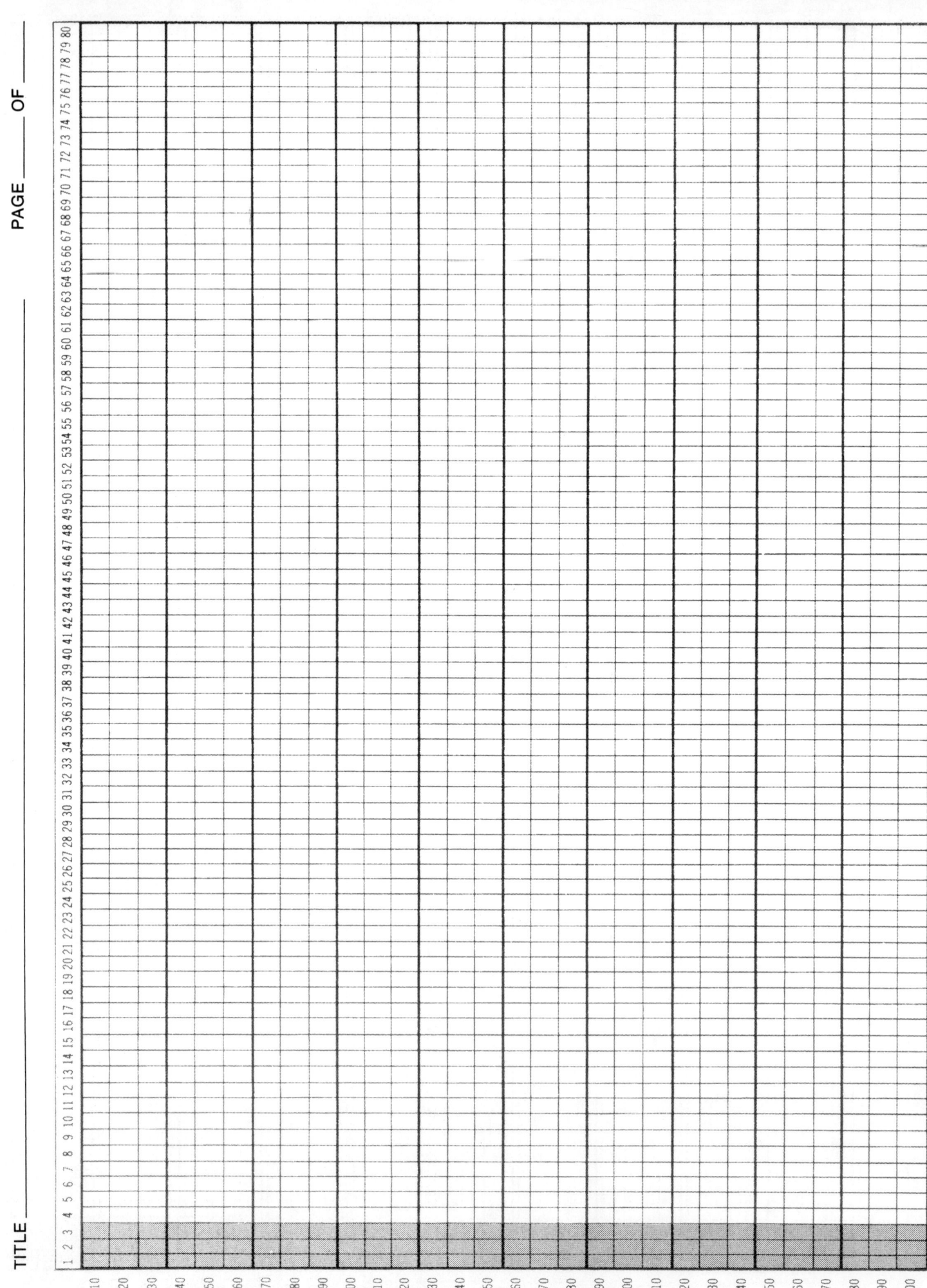

TITLE ______________________________ PAGE ______ OF ______

1 2 3 4 5 6 7 8 9 10 11 12 13 14 15 16 17 18 19 20 21 22 23 24 25 26 27 28 29 30 31 32 33 34 35 36 37 38 39 40 41 42 43 44 45 46 47 48 49 50 51 52 53 54 55 56 57 58 59 60 61 62 63 64 65 66 67 68 69 70 71 72 73 74 75 76 77 78 79 80

10
20
30
40
50
60
70
80
90
100
110
120
130
140
150
160
170
180
190
200
210
220
230
240
250
260
270
280
290
300

TITLE ____________________ PAGE ______ OF ______

1 2 3 4 5 6 7 8 9 10 11 12 13 14 15 16 17 18 19 20 21 22 23 24 25 26 27 28 29 30 31 32 33 34 35 36 37 38 39 40 41 42 43 44 45 46 47 48 49 50 51 52 53 54 55 56 57 58 59 60 61 62 63 64 65 66 67 68 69 70 71 72 73 74 75 76 77 78 79 80

10
20
30
40
50
60
70
80
90
100
110
120
130
140
150
160
170
180
190
200
210
220
230
240
250
260
270
280
290
300

TITLE _____

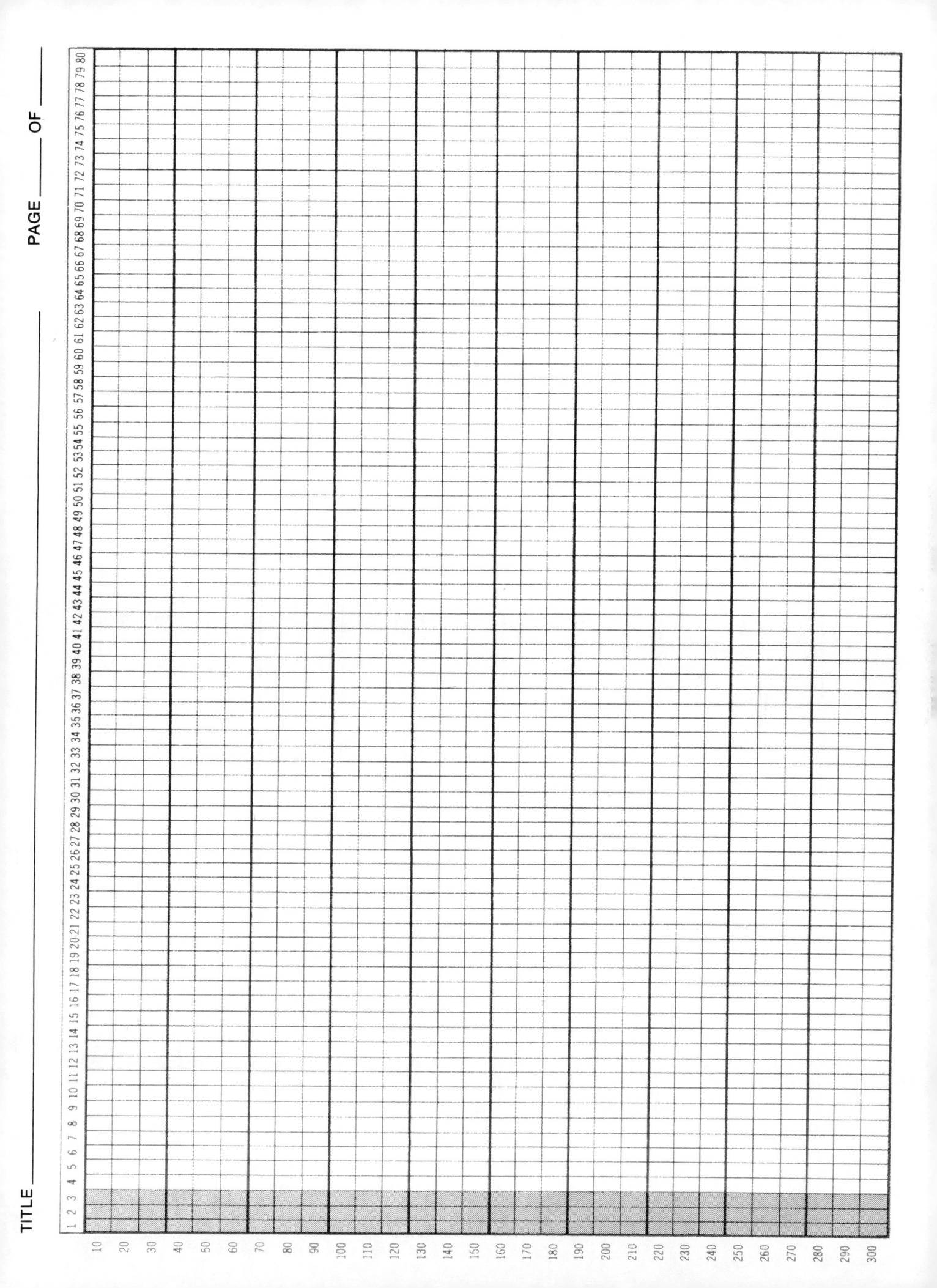

PAGE _____ OF _____

TITLE _____   PAGE ___ OF ___

TITLE ______ PAGE ______ OF ______

1 2 3 4 5 6 7 8 9 10 11 12 13 14 15 16 17 18 19 20 21 22 23 24 25 26 27 28 29 30 31 32 33 34 35 36 37 38 39 40 41 42 43 44 45 46 47 48 49 50 51 52 53 54 55 56 57 58 59 60 61 62 63 64 65 66 67 68 69 70 71 72 73 74 75 76 77 78 79 80

10
20
30
40
50
60
70
80
90
100
110
120
130
140
150
160
170
180
190
200
210
220
230
240
250
260
270
280
290
300

TITLE ______________________ PAGE ______ OF ______

1 2 3 4 5 6 7 8 9 10 11 12 13 14 15 16 17 18 19 20 21 22 23 24 25 26 27 28 29 30 31 32 33 34 35 36 37 38 39 40 41 42 43 44 45 46 47 48 49 50 51 52 53 54 55 56 57 58 59 60 61 62 63 64 65 66 67 68 69 70 71 72 73 74 75 76 77 78 79 80

10
20
30
40
50
60
70
80
90
100
110
120
130
140
150
160
170
180
190
200
210
220
230
240
250
260
270
280
290
300

TITLE ____________________ PAGE ______ OF ______

1 2 3 4 5 6 7 8 9 10 11 12 13 14 15 16 17 18 19 20 21 22 23 24 25 26 27 28 29 30 31 32 33 34 35 36 37 38 39 40 41 42 43 44 45 46 47 48 49 50 51 52 53 54 55 56 57 58 59 60 61 62 63 64 65 66 67 68 69 70 71 72 73 74 75 76 77 78 79 80

10
20
30
40
50
60
70
80
90
100
110
120
130
140
150
160
170
180
190
200
210
220
230
240
250
260
270
280
290
300

TITLE _____   PAGE ____ OF ____

TITLE ____________________ PAGE ______ OF ______

1 2 3 4 5 6 7 8 9 10 11 12 13 14 15 16 17 18 19 20 21 22 23 24 25 26 27 28 29 30 31 32 33 34 35 36 37 38 39 40 41 42 43 44 45 46 47 48 49 50 51 52 53 54 55 56 57 58 59 60 61 62 63 64 65 66 67 68 69 70 71 72 73 74 75 76 77 78 79 80

10
20
30
40
50
60
70
80
90
100
110
120
130
140
150
160
170
180
190
200
210
220
230
240
250
260
270
280
290
300

TITLE ______________________________ PAGE ______ OF ______

1 2 3 4 5 6 7 8 9 10 11 12 13 14 15 16 17 18 19 20 21 22 23 24 25 26 27 28 29 30 31 32 33 34 35 36 37 38 39 40 41 42 43 44 45 46 47 48 49 50 51 52 53 54 55 56 57 58 59 60 61 62 63 64 65 66 67 68 69 70 71 72 73 74 75 76 77 78 79 80

10
20
30
40
50
60
70
80
90
100
110
120
130
140
150
160
170
180
190
200
210
220
230
240
250
260
270
280
290
300

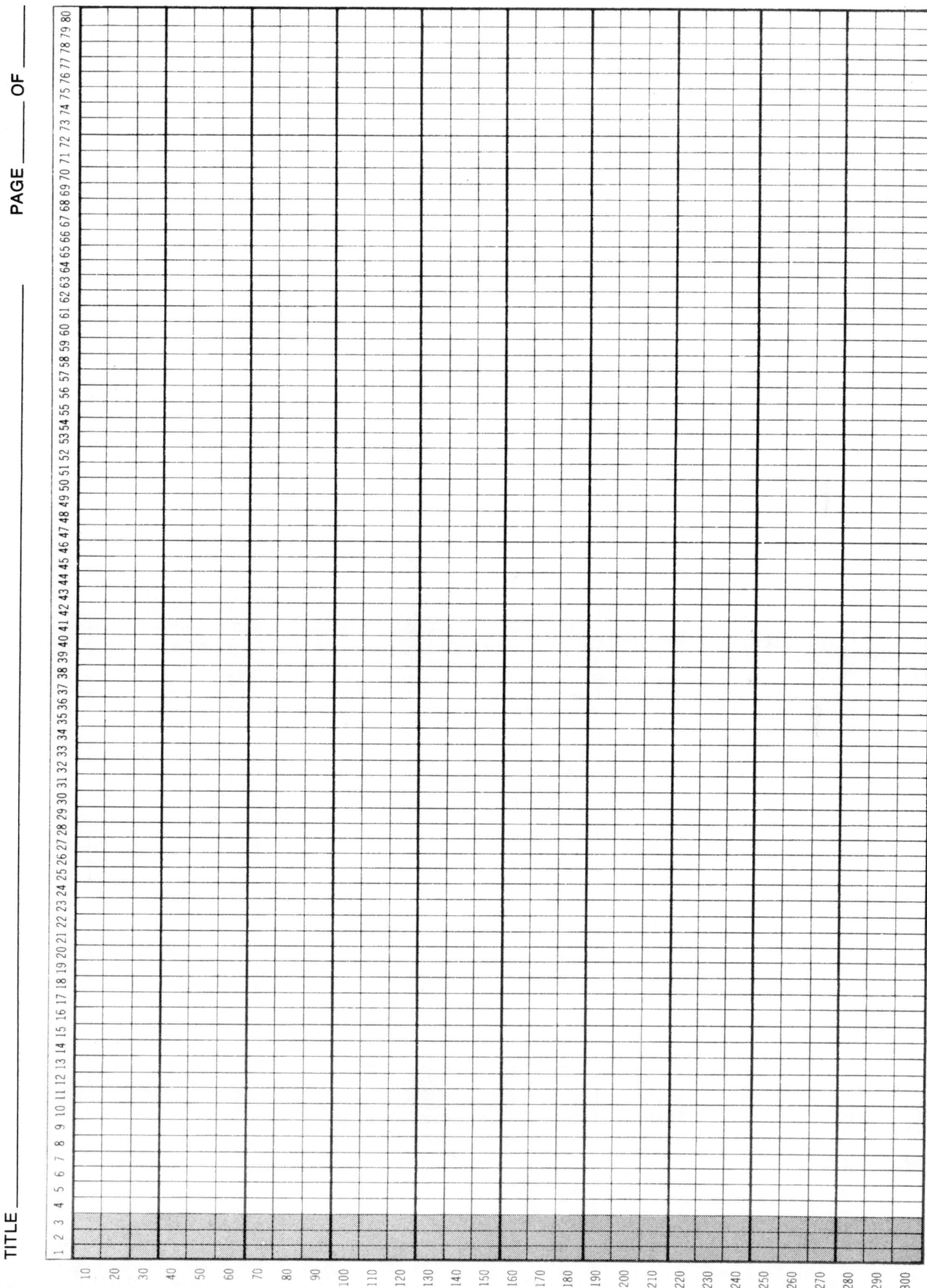

TITLE ______________________________ PAGE ______ OF ______

1 2 3 4 5 6 7 8 9 10 11 12 13 14 15 16 17 18 19 20 21 22 23 24 25 26 27 28 29 30 31 32 33 34 35 36 37 38 39 40 41 42 43 44 45 46 47 48 49 50 51 52 53 54 55 56 57 58 59 60 61 62 63 64 65 66 67 68 69 70 71 72 73 74 75 76 77 78 79 80

10
20
30
40
50
60
70
80
90
100
110
120
130
140
150
160
170
180
190
200
210
220
230
240
250
260
270
280
290
300

TITLE ____________________ PAGE ______ OF ______

1 2 3 4 5 6 7 8 9 10 11 12 13 14 15 16 17 18 19 20 21 22 23 24 25 26 27 28 29 30 31 32 33 34 35 36 37 38 39 40 41 42 43 44 45 46 47 48 49 50 51 52 53 54 55 56 57 58 59 60 61 62 63 64 65 66 67 68 69 70 71 72 73 74 75 76 77 78 79 80

10
20
30
40
50
60
70
80
90
100
110
120
130
140
150
160
170
180
190
200
210
220
230
240
250
260
270
280
290
300

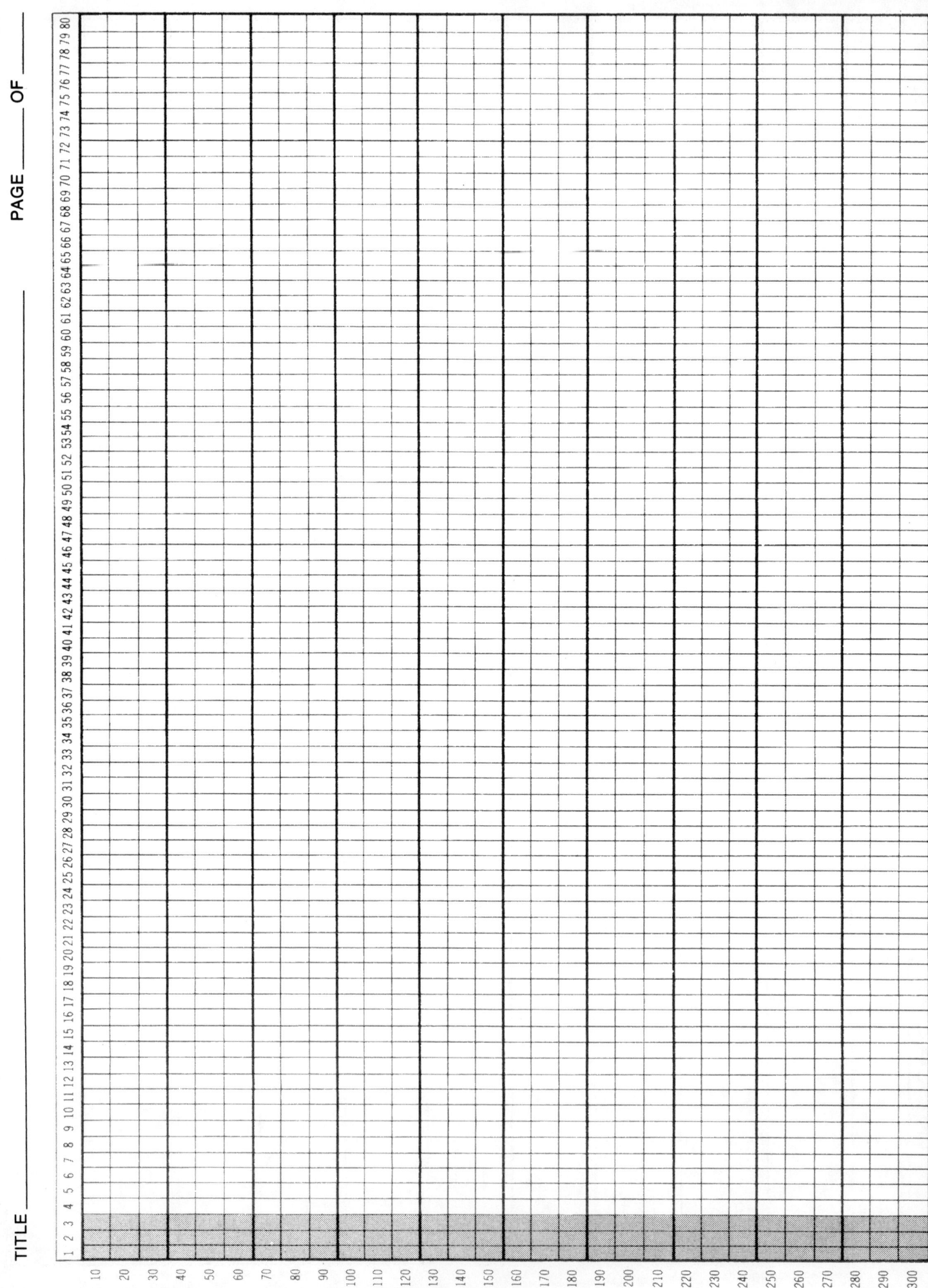

TITLE ______________________________ PAGE ______ OF ______

1 2 3 4 5 6 7 8 9 10 11 12 13 14 15 16 17 18 19 20 21 22 23 24 25 26 27 28 29 30 31 32 33 34 35 36 37 38 39 40 41 42 43 44 45 46 47 48 49 50 51 52 53 54 55 56 57 58 59 60 61 62 63 64 65 66 67 68 69 70 71 72 73 74 75 76 77 78 79 80

10
20
30
40
50
60
70
80
90
100
110
120
130
140
150
160
170
180
190
200
210
220
230
240
250
260
270
280
290
300

TITLE ______________________________ PAGE ______ OF ______

1 2 3 4 5 6 7 8 9 10 11 12 13 14 15 16 17 18 19 20 21 22 23 24 25 26 27 28 29 30 31 32 33 34 35 36 37 38 39 40 41 42 43 44 45 46 47 48 49 50 51 52 53 54 55 56 57 58 59 60 61 62 63 64 65 66 67 68 69 70 71 72 73 74 75 76 77 78 79 80

10
20
30
40
50
60
70
80
90
100
110
120
130
140
150
160
170
180
190
200
210
220
230
240
250
260
270
280
290
300

TITLE ______________________________ PAGE ______ OF ______

1 2 3 4 5 6 7 8 9 10 11 12 13 14 15 16 17 18 19 20 21 22 23 24 25 26 27 28 29 30 31 32 33 34 35 36 37 38 39 40 41 42 43 44 45 46 47 48 49 50 51 52 53 54 55 56 57 58 59 60 61 62 63 64 65 66 67 68 69 70 71 72 73 74 75 76 77 78 79 80

10
20
30
40
50
60
70
80
90
100
110
120
130
140
150
160
170
180
190
200
210
220
230
240
250
260
270
280
290
300

TITLE _____   PAGE ____ OF ____

TITLE ______________________________ PAGE ______ OF ______

1 2 3 4 5 6 7 8 9 10 11 12 13 14 15 16 17 18 19 20 21 22 23 24 25 26 27 28 29 30 31 32 33 34 35 36 37 38 39 40 41 42 43 44 45 46 47 48 49 50 51 52 53 54 55 56 57 58 59 60 61 62 63 64 65 66 67 68 69 70 71 72 73 74 75 76 77 78 79 80

10
20
30
40
50
60
70
80
90
100
110
120
130
140
150
160
170
180
190
200
210
220
230
240
250
260
270
280
290
300

TITLE _____   PAGE ____ OF ____

TITLE ______________________________ PAGE ______ OF ______

1 2 3 4 5 6 7 8 9 10 11 12 13 14 15 16 17 18 19 20 21 22 23 24 25 26 27 28 29 30 31 32 33 34 35 36 37 38 39 40 41 42 43 44 45 46 47 48 49 50 51 52 53 54 55 56 57 58 59 60 61 62 63 64 65 66 67 68 69 70 71 72 73 74 75 76 77 78 79 80

10
20
30
40
50
60
70
80
90
100
110
120
130
140
150
160
170
180
190
200
210
220
230
240
250
260
270
280
290
300

TITLE ______________________________ PAGE ______ OF ______

1 2 3 4 5 6 7 8 9 10 11 12 13 14 15 16 17 18 19 20 21 22 23 24 25 26 27 28 29 30 31 32 33 34 35 36 37 38 39 40 41 42 43 44 45 46 47 48 49 50 51 52 53 54 55 56 57 58 59 60 61 62 63 64 65 66 67 68 69 70 71 72 73 74 75 76 77 78 79 80

10
20
30
40
50
60
70
80
90
100
110
120
130
140
150
160
170
180
190
200
210
220
230
240
250
260
270
280
290
300

TITLE _____ PAGE ____ OF ____

TITLE ______ PAGE ______ OF ______

	1	2	3	4	5	6	7	8	9	10	11	12	13	14	15	16	17	18	19	20	21	22	23	24	25	26	27	28	29	30	31	32	33	34	35	36	37	38	39	40	41	42	43	44	45	46	47	48	49	50	51	52	53	54	55	56	57	58	59	60	61	62	63	64	65	66	67	68	69	70	71	72	73	74	75	76	77	78	79	80
10																																																																																
20																																																																																
30																																																																																
40																																																																																
50																																																																																
60																																																																																
70																																																																																
80																																																																																
90																																																																																
100																																																																																
110																																																																																
120																																																																																
130																																																																																
140																																																																																
150																																																																																
160																																																																																
170																																																																																
180																																																																																
190																																																																																
200																																																																																
210																																																																																
220																																																																																
230																																																																																
240																																																																																
250																																																																																
260																																																																																
270																																																																																
280																																																																																
290																																																																																
300																																																																																

TITLE _____   PAGE _____ OF _____

TITLE ____________________ PAGE ______ OF ______

1 2 3 4 5 6 7 8 9 10 11 12 13 14 15 16 17 18 19 20 21 22 23 24 25 26 27 28 29 30 31 32 33 34 35 36 37 38 39 40 41 42 43 44 45 46 47 48 49 50 51 52 53 54 55 56 57 58 59 60 61 62 63 64 65 66 67 68 69 70 71 72 73 74 75 76 77 78 79 80

10
20
30
40
50
60
70
80
90
100
110
120
130
140
150
160
170
180
190
200
210
220
230
240
250
260
270
280
290
300

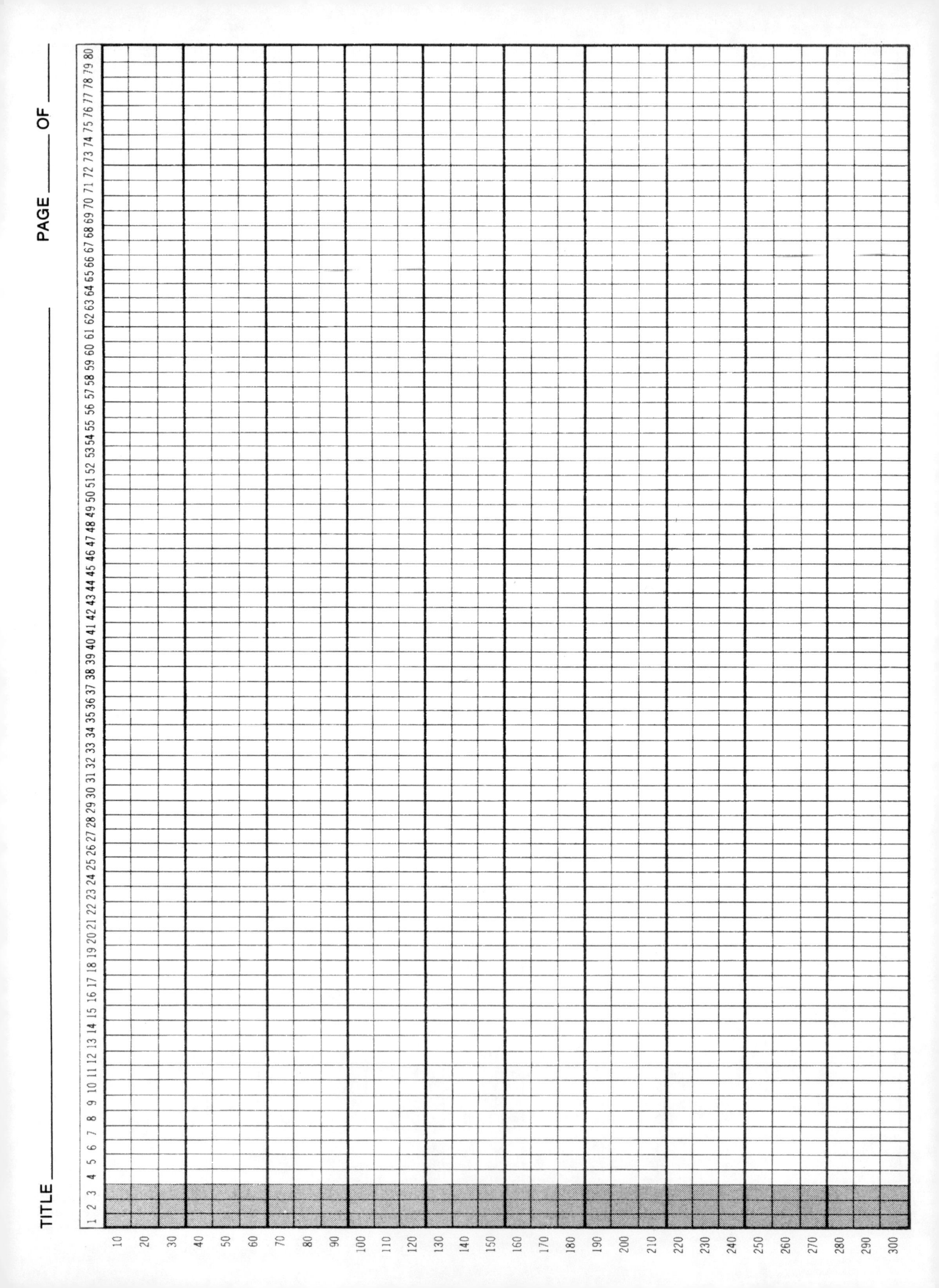

TITLE ____________________ PAGE ______ OF ______

1 2 3 4 5 6 7 8 9 10 11 12 13 14 15 16 17 18 19 20 21 22 23 24 25 26 27 28 29 30 31 32 33 34 35 36 37 38 39 40 41 42 43 44 45 46 47 48 49 50 51 52 53 54 55 56 57 58 59 60 61 62 63 64 65 66 67 68 69 70 71 72 73 74 75 76 77 78 79 80

10
20
30
40
50
60
70
80
90
100
110
120
130
140
150
160
170
180
190
200
210
220
230
240
250
260
270
280
290
300

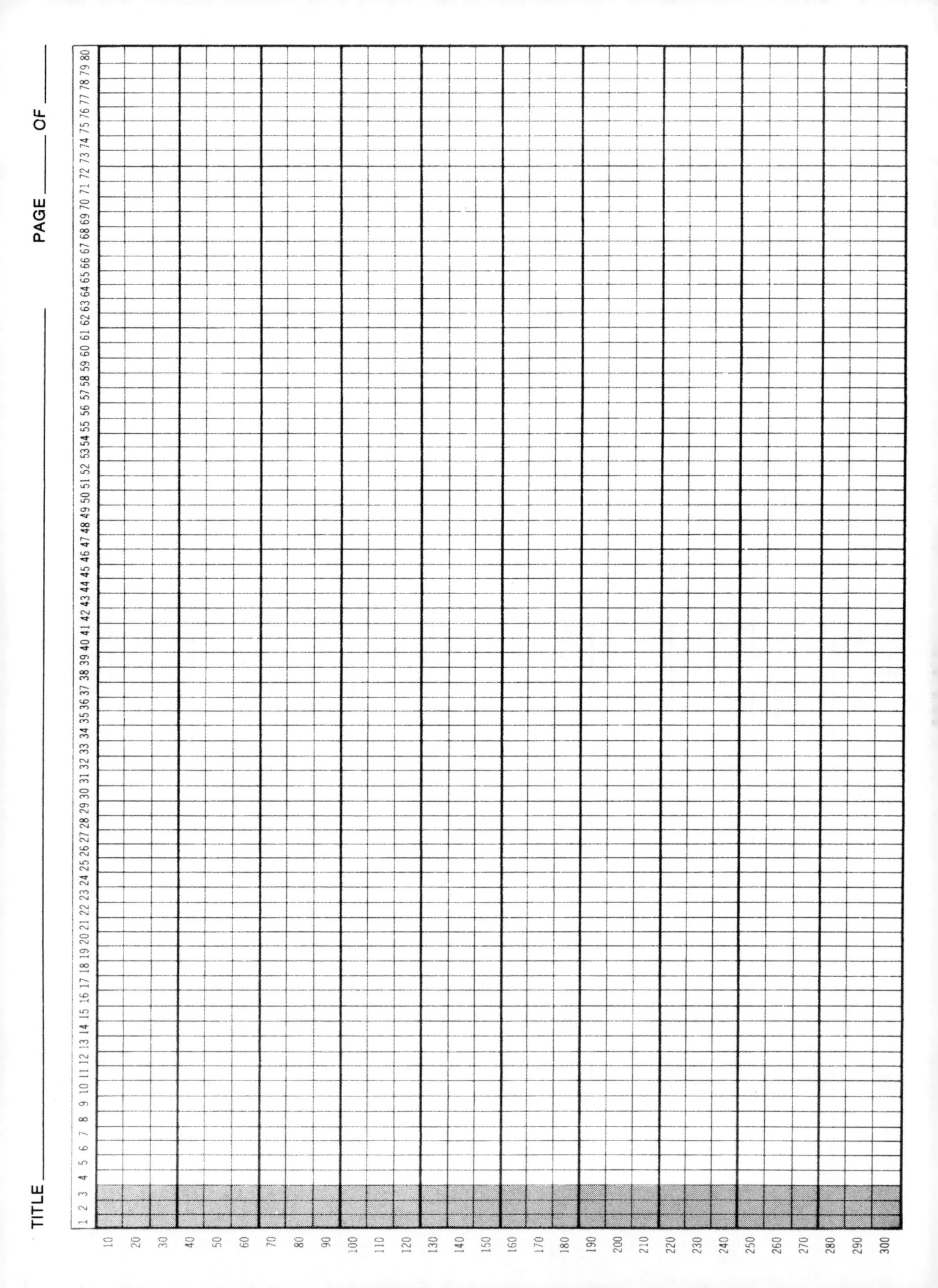

TITLE ______________________________ PAGE ______ OF ______

1 2 3 4 5 6 7 8 9 10 11 12 13 14 15 16 17 18 19 20 21 22 23 24 25 26 27 28 29 30 31 32 33 34 35 36 37 38 39 40 41 42 43 44 45 46 47 48 49 50 51 52 53 54 55 56 57 58 59 60 61 62 63 64 65 66 67 68 69 70 71 72 73 74 75 76 77 78 79 80

10
20
30
40
50
60
70
80
90
100
110
120
130
140
150
160
170
180
190
200
210
220
230
240
250
260
270
280
290
300

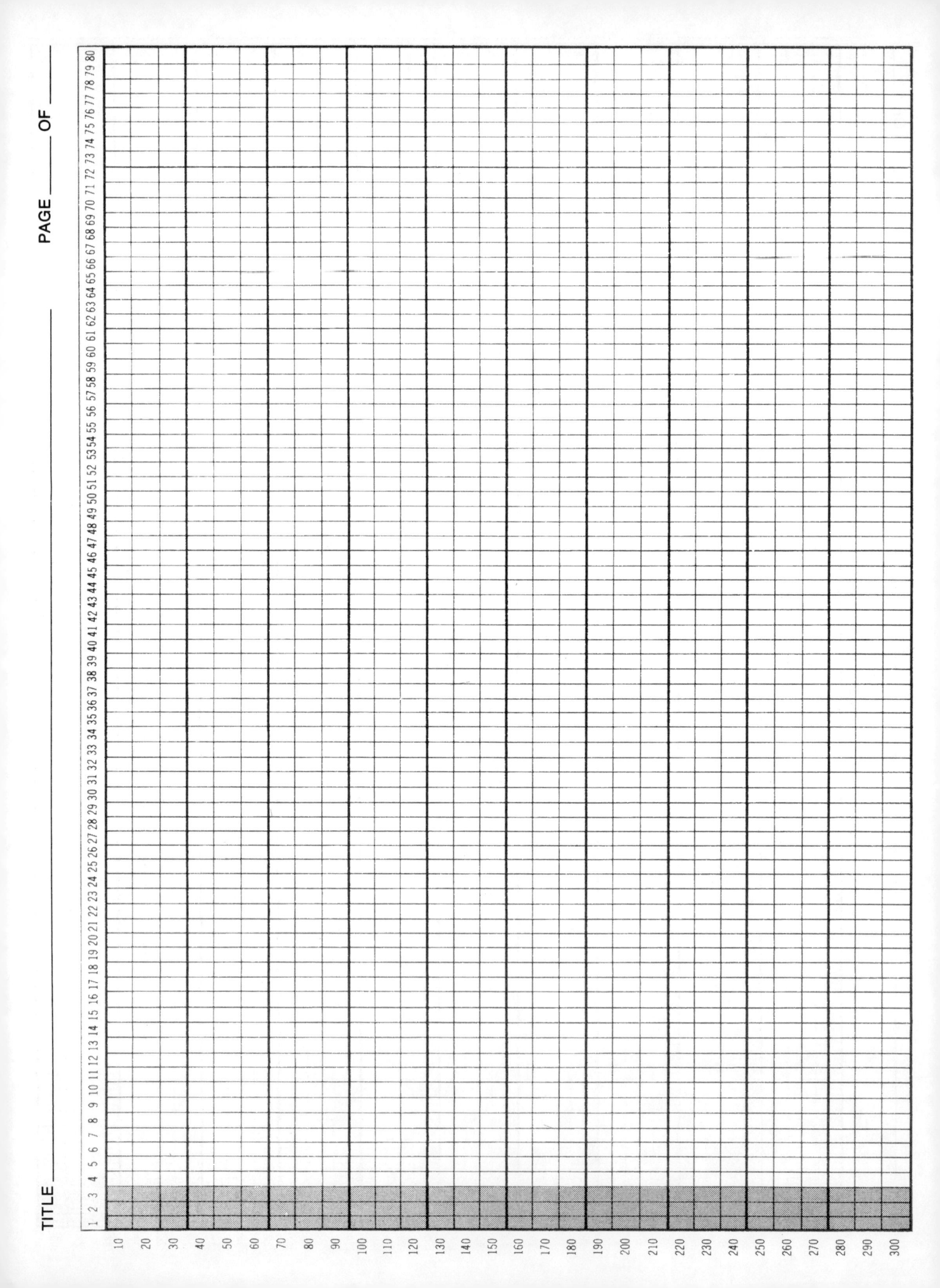

TITLE ______________________ PAGE ______ OF ______

1 2 3 4 5 6 7 8 9 10 11 12 13 14 15 16 17 18 19 20 21 22 23 24 25 26 27 28 29 30 31 32 33 34 35 36 37 38 39 40 41 42 43 44 45 46 47 48 49 50 51 52 53 54 55 56 57 58 59 60 61 62 63 64 65 66 67 68 69 70 71 72 73 74 75 76 77 78 79 80

10
20
30
40
50
60
70
80
90
100
110
120
130
140
150
160
170
180
190
200
210
220
230
240
250
260
270
280
290
300

TITLE _____   PAGE ____ OF ____

TITLE _____ PAGE ____ OF ____

TITLE ____________________ PAGE ______ OF ______

1 2 3 4 5 6 7 8 9 10 11 12 13 14 15 16 17 18 19 20 21 22 23 24 25 26 27 28 29 30 31 32 33 34 35 36 37 38 39 40 41 42 43 44 45 46 47 48 49 50 51 52 53 54 55 56 57 58 59 60 61 62 63 64 65 66 67 68 69 70 71 72 73 74 75 76 77 78 79 80

10
20
30
40
50
60
70
80
90
100
110
120
130
140
150
160
170
180
190
200
210
220
230
240
250
260
270
280
290
300

TITLE ____________________ PAGE ______ OF ______

1 2 3 4 5 6 7 8 9 10 11 12 13 14 15 16 17 18 19 20 21 22 23 24 25 26 27 28 29 30 31 32 33 34 35 36 37 38 39 40 41 42 43 44 45 46 47 48 49 50 51 52 53 54 55 56 57 58 59 60 61 62 63 64 65 66 67 68 69 70 71 72 73 74 75 76 77 78 79 80

10
20
30
40
50
60
70
80
90
100
110
120
130
140
150
160
170
180
190
200
210
220
230
240
250
260
270
280
290
300

TITLE ______________________________ PAGE ______ OF ______

1 2 3 4 5 6 7 8 9 10 11 12 13 14 15 16 17 18 19 20 21 22 23 24 25 26 27 28 29 30 31 32 33 34 35 36 37 38 39 40 41 42 43 44 45 46 47 48 49 50 51 52 53 54 55 56 57 58 59 60 61 62 63 64 65 66 67 68 69 70 71 72 73 74 75 76 77 78 79 80

10
20
30
40
50
60
70
80
90
100
110
120
130
140
150
160
170
180
190
200
210
220
230
240
250
260
270
280
290
300

TITLE _____ PAGE ____ OF ____

TITLE ______________________________ PAGE ______ OF ______

1 2 3 4 5 6 7 8 9 10 11 12 13 14 15 16 17 18 19 20 21 22 23 24 25 26 27 28 29 30 31 32 33 34 35 36 37 38 39 40 41 42 43 44 45 46 47 48 49 50 51 52 53 54 55 56 57 58 59 60 61 62 63 64 65 66 67 68 69 70 71 72 73 74 75 76 77 78 79 80

10
20
30
40
50
60
70
80
90
100
110
120
130
140
150
160
170
180
190
200
210
220
230
240
250
260
270
280
290
300

TITLE _____ PAGE ____ OF ____

TITLE ______________________ PAGE ______ OF ______

1 2 3 4 5 6 7 8 9 10 11 12 13 14 15 16 17 18 19 20 21 22 23 24 25 26 27 28 29 30 31 32 33 34 35 36 37 38 39 40 41 42 43 44 45 46 47 48 49 50 51 52 53 54 55 56 57 58 59 60 61 62 63 64 65 66 67 68 69 70 71 72 73 74 75 76 77 78 79 80

10
20
30
40
50
60
70
80
90
100
110
120
130
140
150
160
170
180
190
200
210
220
230
240
250
260
270
280
290
300

TITLE ____________________ PAGE ______ OF ______

	1	2	3	4	5	6	7	8	9	10	11	12	13	14	15	16	17	18	19	20	21	22	23	24	25	26	27	28	29	30	31	32	33	34	35	36	37	38	39	40	41	42	43	44	45	46	47	48	49	50	51	52	53	54	55	56	57	58	59	60	61	62	63	64	65	66	67	68	69	70	71	72	73	74	75	76	77	78	79	80
10
20
30
40
50
60
70
80
90
100
110
120
130
140
150
160
170
180
190
200
210
220
230
240
250
260
270
280
290
300

TITLE ______________________________ PAGE ______ OF ______

	1	2	3	4	5	6	7	8	9	10	11	12	13	14	15	16	17	18	19	20	21	22	23	24	25	26	27	28	29	30	31	32	33	34	35	36	37	38	39	40	41	42	43	44	45	46	47	48	49	50	51	52	53	54	55	56	57	58	59	60	61	62	63	64	65	66	67	68	69	70	71	72	73	74	75	76	77	78	79	80
10																																																																															
20																																																																															
30																																																																															
40																																																																															
50																																																																															
60																																																																															
70																																																																															
80																																																																															
90																																																																															
100																																																																															
110																																																																															
120																																																																															
130																																																																															
140																																																																															
150																																																																															
160																																																																															
170																																																																															
180																																																																															
190																																																																															
200																																																																															
210																																																																															
220																																																																															
230																																																																															
240																																																																															
250																																																																															
260																																																																															
270																																																																															
280																																																																															
290																																																																															
300																																																																															

TITLE ____________________ PAGE ______ OF ______

1 2 3 4 5 6 7 8 9 10 11 12 13 14 15 16 17 18 19 20 21 22 23 24 25 26 27 28 29 30 31 32 33 34 35 36 37 38 39 40 41 42 43 44 45 46 47 48 49 50 51 52 53 54 55 56 57 58 59 60 61 62 63 64 65 66 67 68 69 70 71 72 73 74 75 76 77 78 79 80

10
20
30
40
50
60
70
80
90
100
110
120
130
140
150
160
170
180
190
200
210
220
230
240
250
260
270
280
290
300

TITLE ____________________ PAGE ______ OF ______

1 2 3 4 5 6 7 8 9 10 11 12 13 14 15 16 17 18 19 20 21 22 23 24 25 26 27 28 29 30 31 32 33 34 35 36 37 38 39 40 41 42 43 44 45 46 47 48 49 50 51 52 53 54 55 56 57 58 59 60 61 62 63 64 65 66 67 68 69 70 71 72 73 74 75 76 77 78 79 80

10
20
30
40
50
60
70
80
90
100
110
120
130
140
150
160
170
180
190
200
210
220
230
240
250
260
270
280
290
300

TITLE ______________________ PAGE ______ OF ______

1 2 3 4 5 6 7 8 9 10 11 12 13 14 15 16 17 18 19 20 21 22 23 24 25 26 27 28 29 30 31 32 33 34 35 36 37 38 39 40 41 42 43 44 45 46 47 48 49 50 51 52 53 54 55 56 57 58 59 60 61 62 63 64 65 66 67 68 69 70 71 72 73 74 75 76 77 78 79 80

10
20
30
40
50
60
70
80
90
100
110
120
130
140
150
160
170
180
190
200
210
220
230
240
250
260
270
280
290
300

TITLE ____________________ PAGE ______ OF ______

1 2 3 4 5 6 7 8 9 10 11 12 13 14 15 16 17 18 19 20 21 22 23 24 25 26 27 28 29 30 31 32 33 34 35 36 37 38 39 40 41 42 43 44 45 46 47 48 49 50 51 52 53 54 55 56 57 58 59 60 61 62 63 64 65 66 67 68 69 70 71 72 73 74 75 76 77 78 79 80

10
20
30
40
50
60
70
80
90
100
110
120
130
140
150
160
170
180
190
200
210
220
230
240
250
260
270
280
290
300

TITLE ______________________________ PAGE ______ OF ______

1 2 3 4 5 6 7 8 9 10 11 12 13 14 15 16 17 18 19 20 21 22 23 24 25 26 27 28 29 30 31 32 33 34 35 36 37 38 39 40 41 42 43 44 45 46 47 48 49 50 51 52 53 54 55 56 57 58 59 60 61 62 63 64 65 66 67 68 69 70 71 72 73 74 75 76 77 78 79 80

10
20
30
40
50
60
70
80
90
100
110
120
130
140
150
160
170
180
190
200
210
220
230
240
250
260
270
280
290
300

TITLE ______________________________ PAGE ______ OF ______

	1	2	3	4	5	6	7	8	9	10	11	12	13	14	15	16	17	18	19	20	21	22	23	24	25	26	27	28	29	30	31	32	33	34	35	36	37	38	39	40	41	42	43	44	45	46	47	48	49	50	51	52	53	54	55	56	57	58	59	60	61	62	63	64	65	66	67	68	69	70	71	72	73	74	75	76	77	78	79	80
10																																																																																
20																																																																																
30																																																																																
40																																																																																
50																																																																																
60																																																																																
70																																																																																
80																																																																																
90																																																																																
100																																																																																
110																																																																																
120																																																																																
130																																																																																
140																																																																																
150																																																																																
160																																																																																
170																																																																																
180																																																																																
190																																																																																
200																																																																																
210																																																																																
220																																																																																
230																																																																																
240																																																																																
250																																																																																
260																																																																																
270																																																																																
280																																																																																
290																																																																																
300																																																																																

TITLE ______________________________ PAGE ______ OF ______

1 2 3 4 5 6 7 8 9 10 11 12 13 14 15 16 17 18 19 20 21 22 23 24 25 26 27 28 29 30 31 32 33 34 35 36 37 38 39 40 41 42 43 44 45 46 47 48 49 50 51 52 53 54 55 56 57 58 59 60 61 62 63 64 65 66 67 68 69 70 71 72 73 74 75 76 77 78 79 80

10
20
30
40
50
60
70
80
90
100
110
120
130
140
150
160
170
180
190
200
210
220
230
240
250
260
270
280
290
300

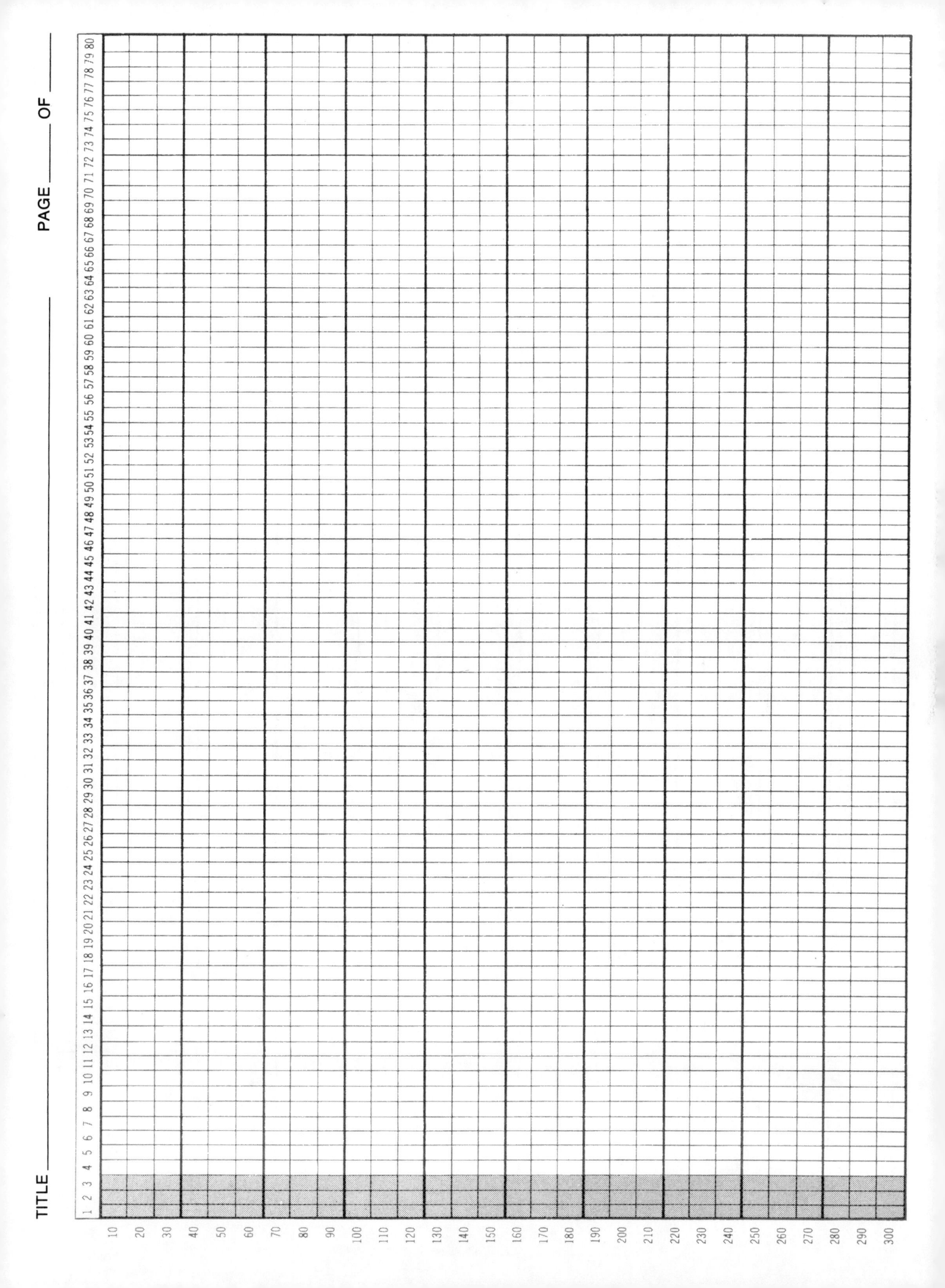

TITLE ____________________ PAGE ______ OF ______

1 2 3 4 5 6 7 8 9 10 11 12 13 14 15 16 17 18 19 20 21 22 23 24 25 26 27 28 29 30 31 32 33 34 35 36 37 38 39 40 41 42 43 44 45 46 47 48 49 50 51 52 53 54 55 56 57 58 59 60 61 62 63 64 65 66 67 68 69 70 71 72 73 74 75 76 77 78 79 80

10
20
30
40
50
60
70
80
90
100
110
120
130
140
150
160
170
180
190
200
210
220
230
240
250
260
270
280
290
300

TITLE ____________________ PAGE ______ OF ______

1 2 3 4 5 6 7 8 9 10 11 12 13 14 15 16 17 18 19 20 21 22 23 24 25 26 27 28 29 30 31 32 33 34 35 36 37 38 39 40 41 42 43 44 45 46 47 48 49 50 51 52 53 54 55 56 57 58 59 60 61 62 63 64 65 66 67 68 69 70 71 72 73 74 75 76 77 78 79 80

10
20
30
40
50
60
70
80
90
100
110
120
130
140
150
160
170
180
190
200
210
220
230
240
250
260
270
280
290
300

TITLE ______________________________ PAGE ______ OF ______

	1	2	3	4	5	6	7	8	9	10	11	12	13	14	15	16	17	18	19	20	21	22	23	24	25	26	27	28	29	30	31	32	33	34	35	36	37	38	39	40	41	42	43	44	45	46	47	48	49	50	51	52	53	54	55	56	57	58	59	60	61	62	63	64	65	66	67	68	69	70	71	72	73	74	75	76	77	78	79	80
10																																																																															
20																																																																															
30																																																																															
40																																																																															
50																																																																															
60																																																																																
70																																																																															
80																																																																															
90																																																																															
100																																																																															
110																																																																															
120																																																																															
130																																																																															
140																																																																															
150																																																																															
160																																																																															
170																																																																															
180																																																																															
190																																																																															
200																																																																															
210																																																																															
220																																																																															
230																																																																															
240																																																																															
250																																																																															
260																																																																															
270																																																																															
280																																																																															
290																																																																															
300																																																																															

TITLE _____ PAGE ____ OF ____

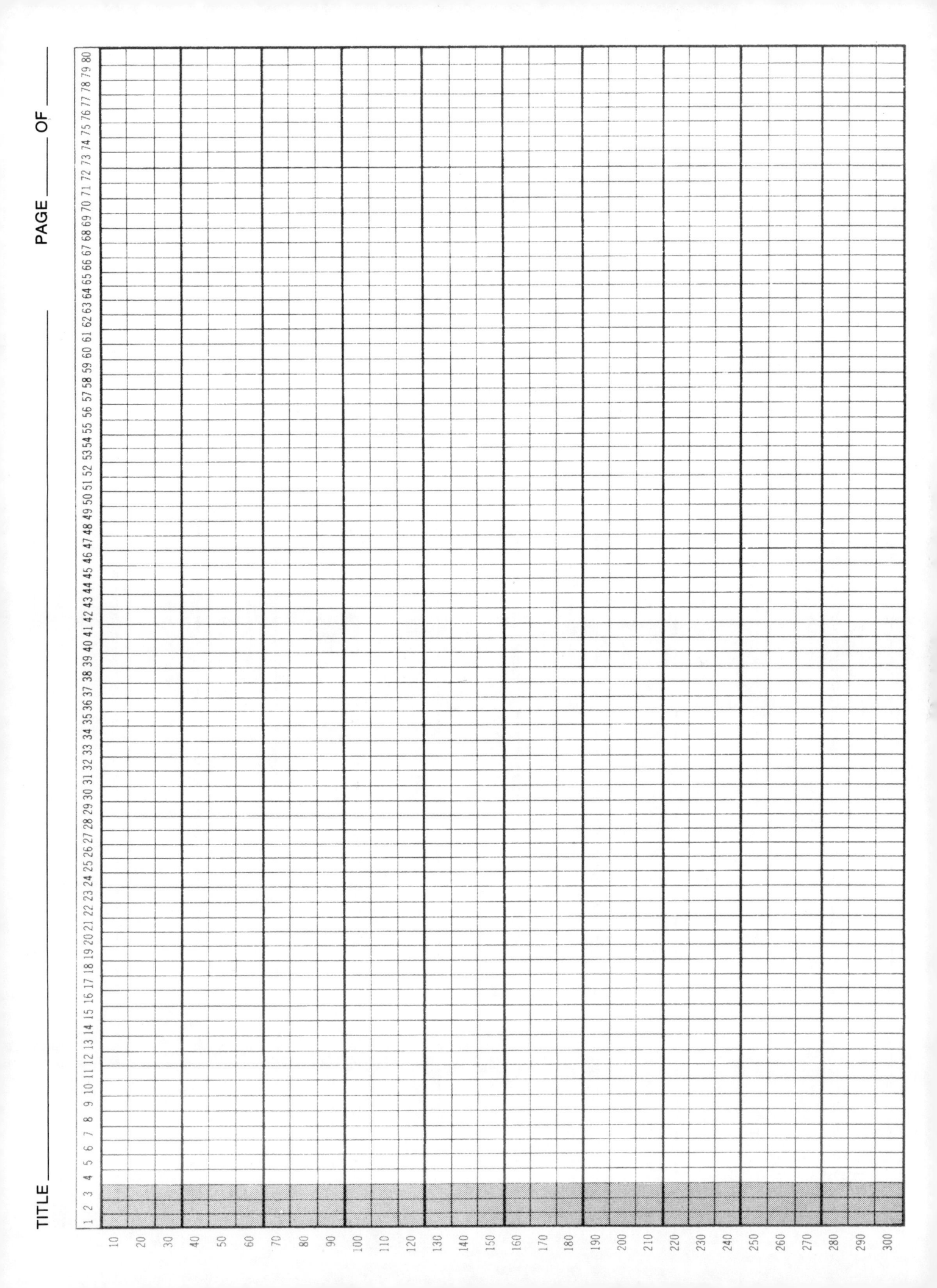

TITLE ______________________________ PAGE ______ OF ______

1 2 3 4 5 6 7 8 9 10 11 12 13 14 15 16 17 18 19 20 21 22 23 24 25 26 27 28 29 30 31 32 33 34 35 36 37 38 39 40 41 42 43 44 45 46 47 48 49 50 51 52 53 54 55 56 57 58 59 60 61 62 63 64 65 66 67 68 69 70 71 72 73 74 75 76 77 78 79 80

10
20
30
40
50
60
70
80
90
100
110
120
130
140
150
160
170
180
190
200
210
220
230
240
250
260
270
280
290
300

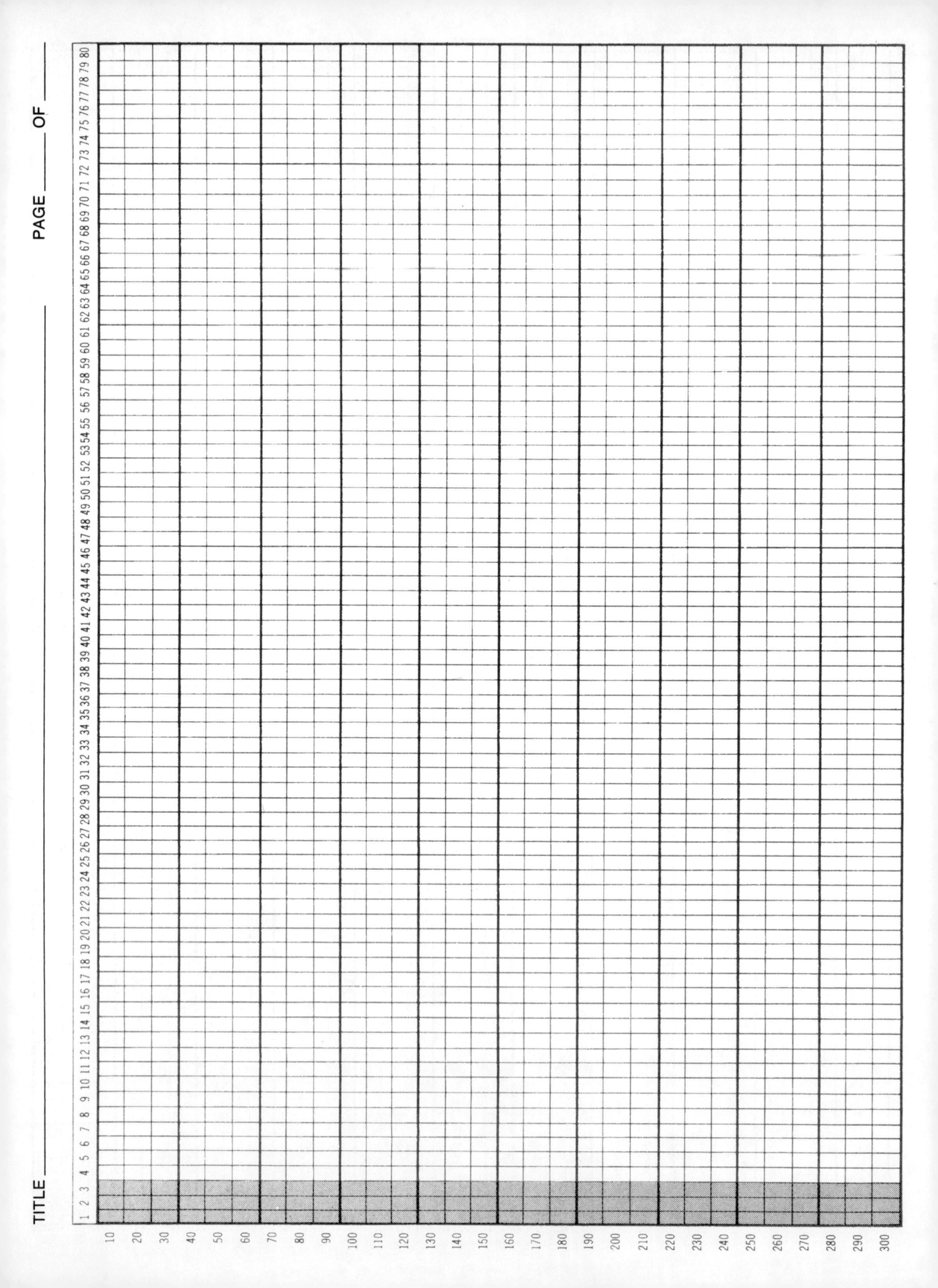

TITLE _____

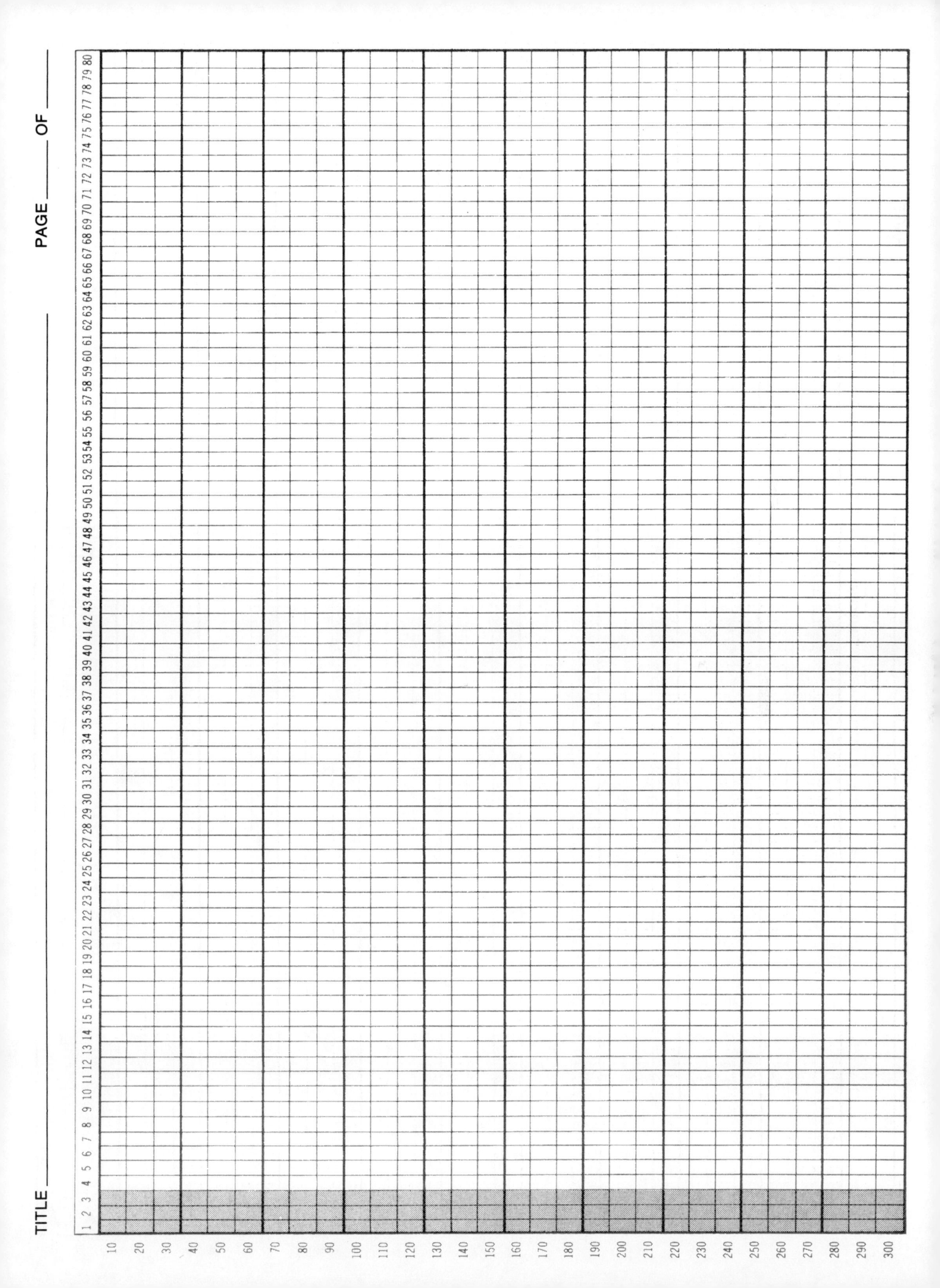

PAGE ____ OF ____

TITLE ______________________________ PAGE ______ OF ______

1 2 3 4 5 6 7 8 9 10 11 12 13 14 15 16 17 18 19 20 21 22 23 24 25 26 27 28 29 30 31 32 33 34 35 36 37 38 39 40 41 42 43 44 45 46 47 48 49 50 51 52 53 54 55 56 57 58 59 60 61 62 63 64 65 66 67 68 69 70 71 72 73 74 75 76 77 78 79 80

10
20
30
40
50
60
70
80
90
100
110
120
130
140
150
160
170
180
190
200
210
220
230
240
250
260
270
280
290
300

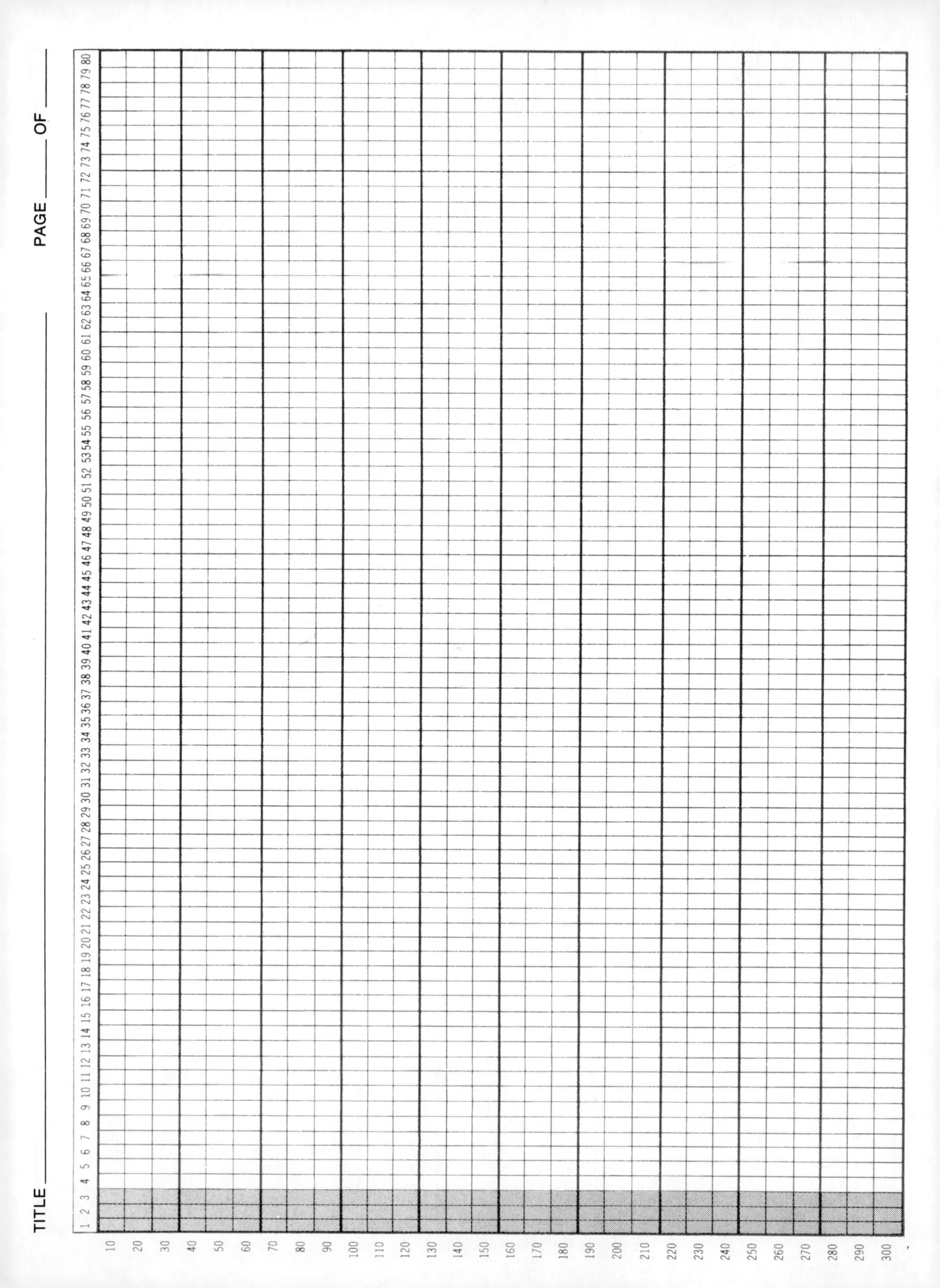

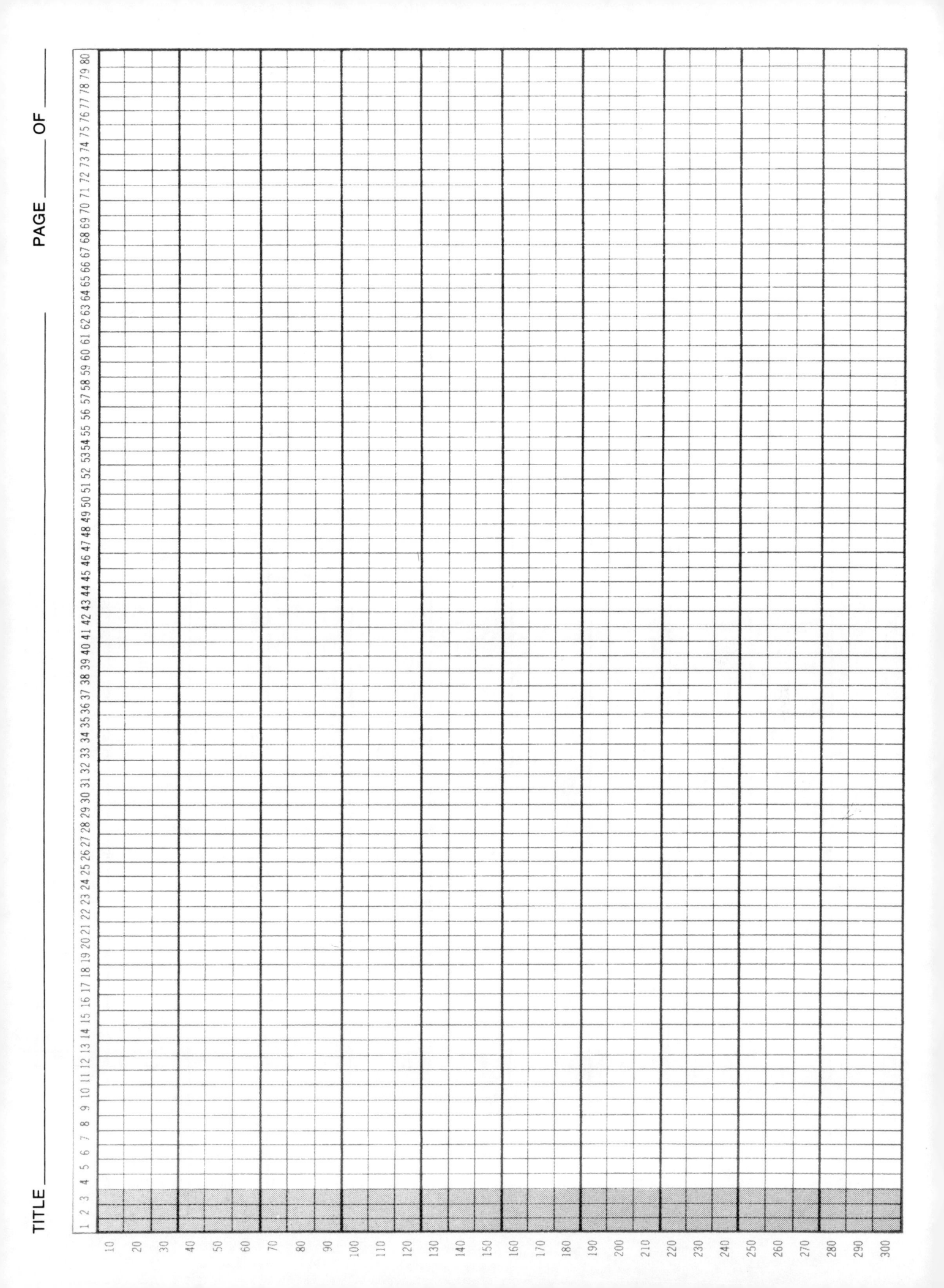

TITLE _____ PAGE _____ OF _____

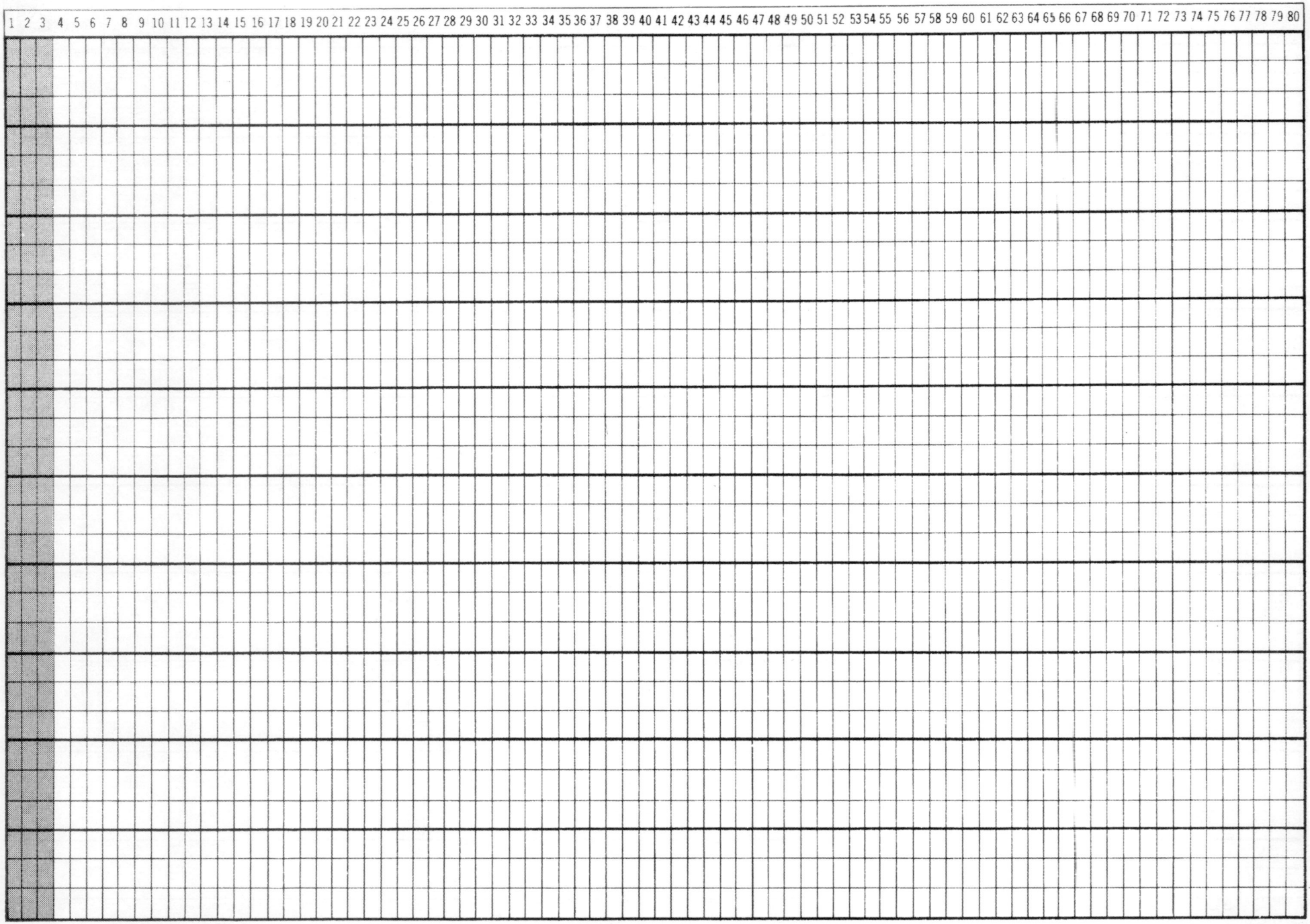

TITLE _____ PAGE ____ OF ____

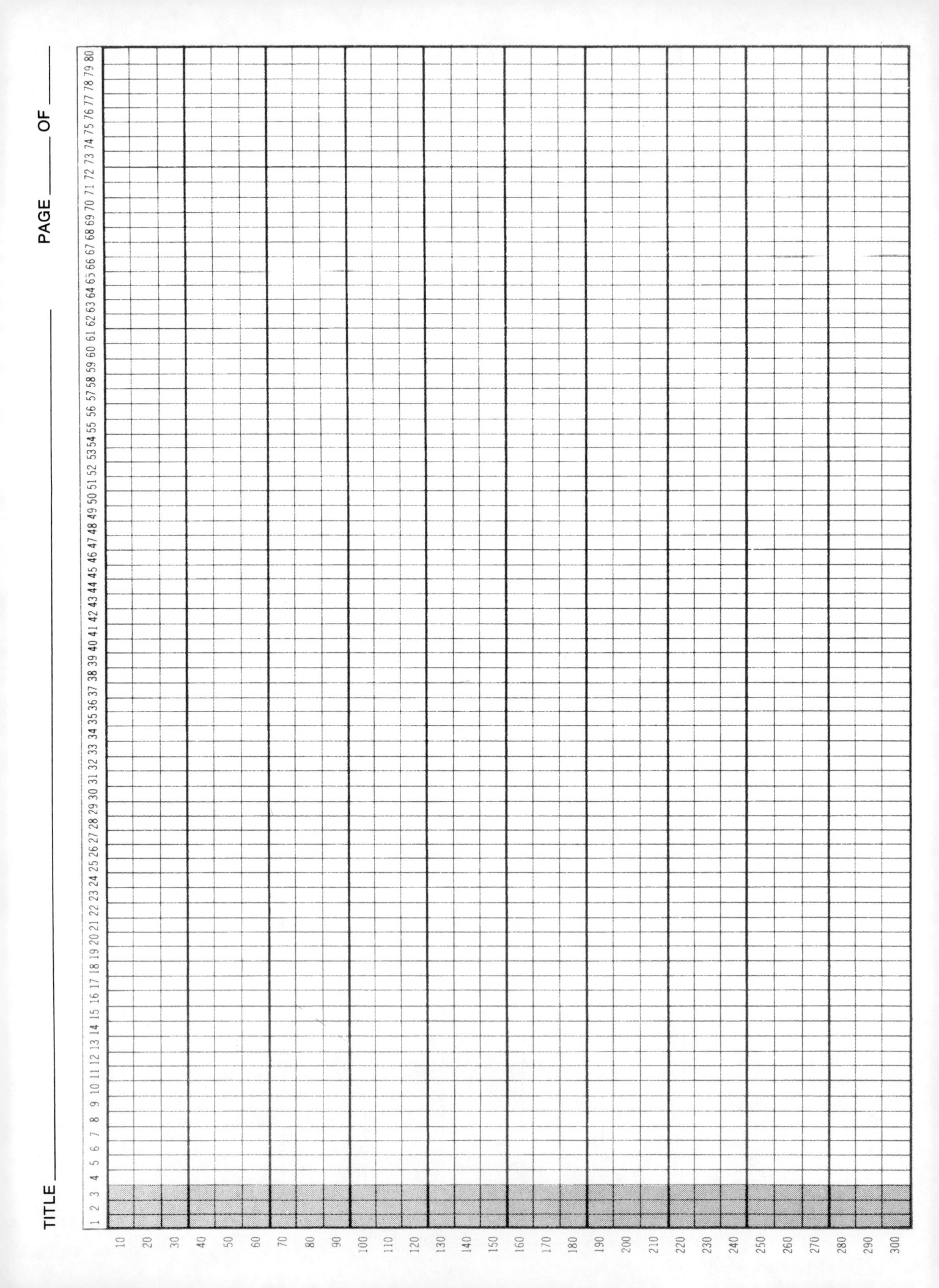

TITLE ______________________________ PAGE ______ OF ______

1 2 3 4 5 6 7 8 9 10 11 12 13 14 15 16 17 18 19 20 21 22 23 24 25 26 27 28 29 30 31 32 33 34 35 36 37 38 39 40 41 42 43 44 45 46 47 48 49 50 51 52 53 54 55 56 57 58 59 60 61 62 63 64 65 66 67 68 69 70 71 72 73 74 75 76 77 78 79 80

10
20
30
40
50
60
70
80
90
100
110
120
130
140
150
160
170
180
190
200
210
220
230
240
250
260
270
280
290
300

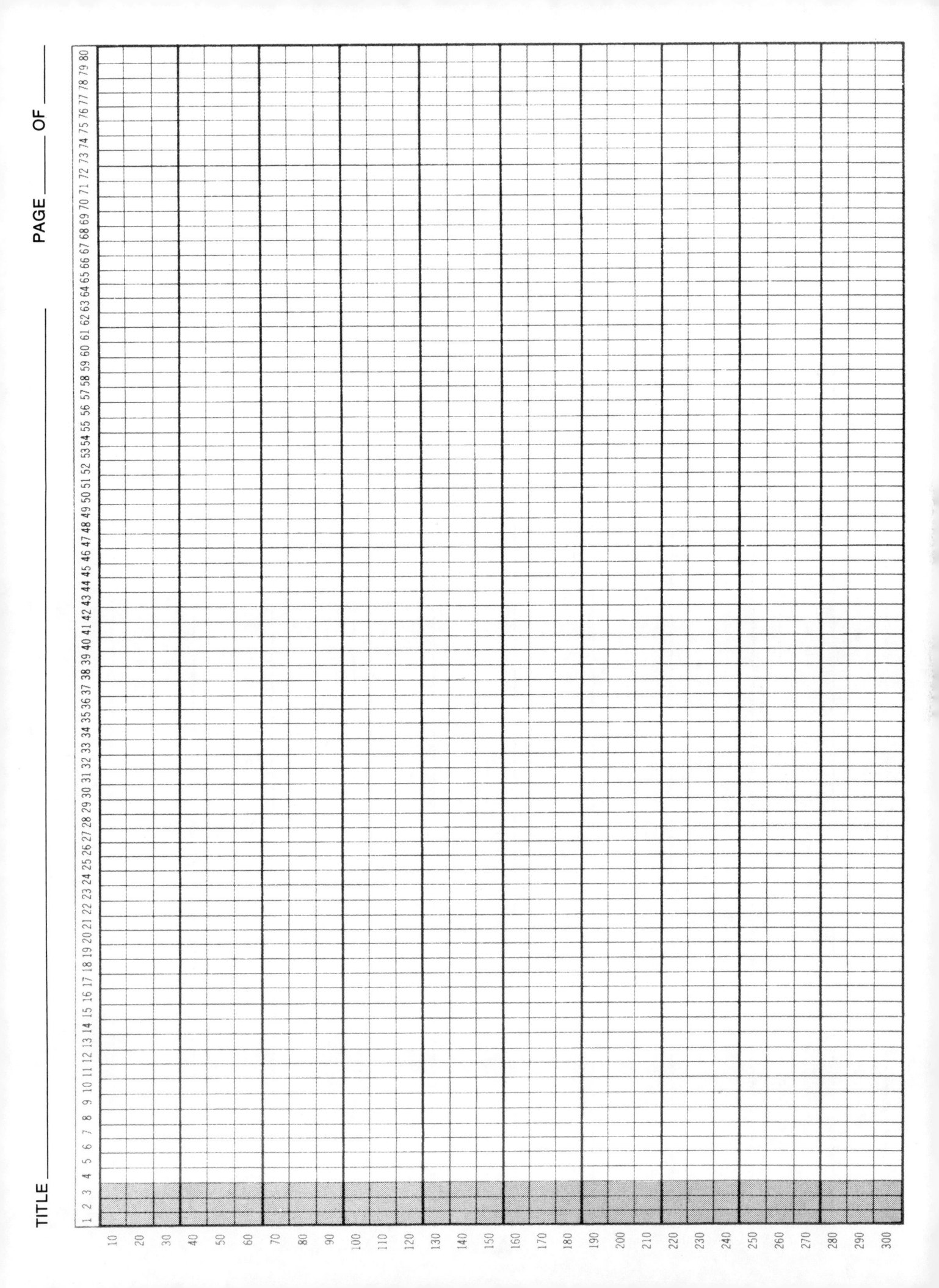

TITLE _____   PAGE ____ OF ____

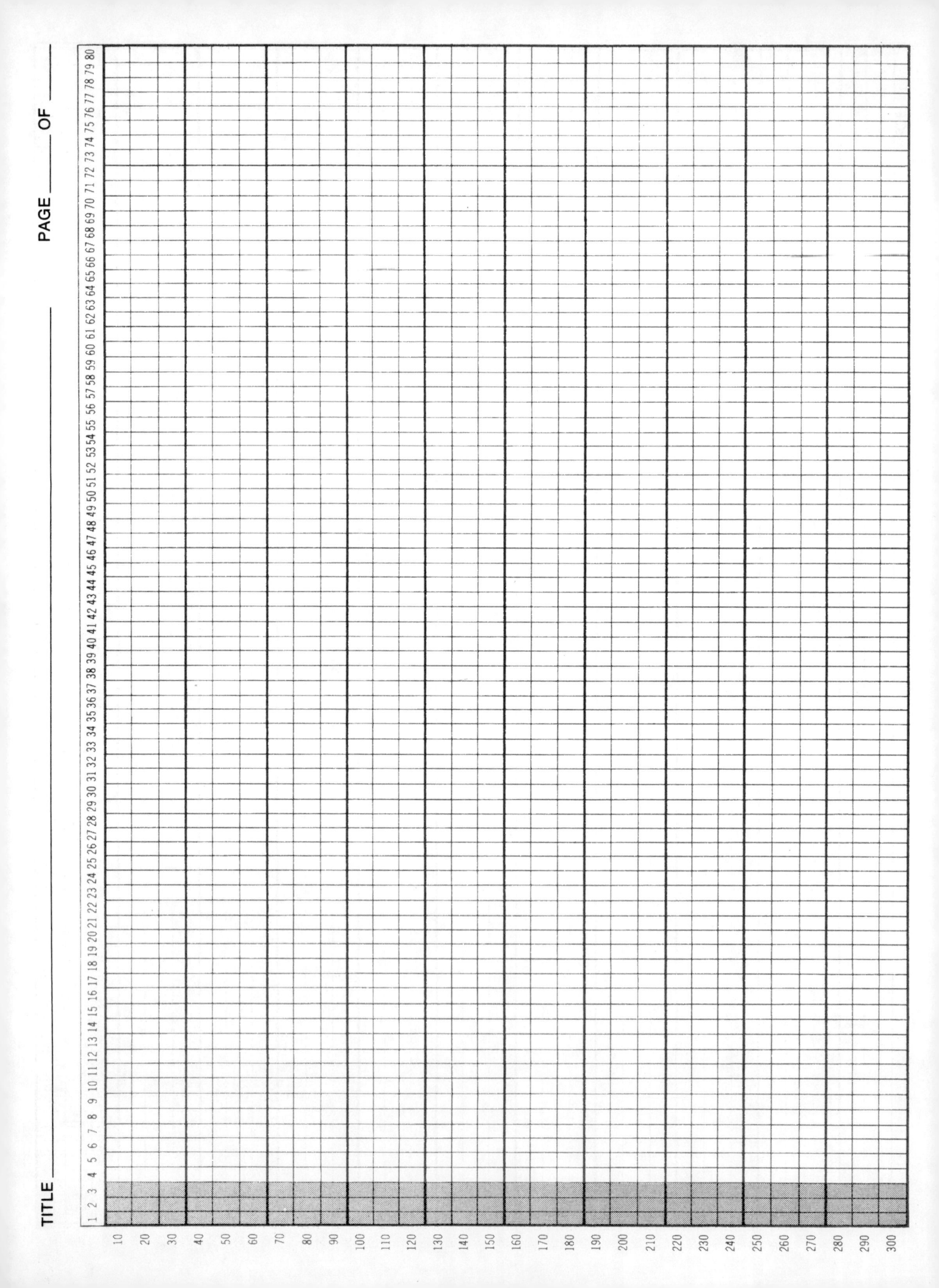

TITLE ____________________ PAGE ______ OF ______

1 2 3 4 5 6 7 8 9 10 11 12 13 14 15 16 17 18 19 20 21 22 23 24 25 26 27 28 29 30 31 32 33 34 35 36 37 38 39 40 41 42 43 44 45 46 47 48 49 50 51 52 53 54 55 56 57 58 59 60 61 62 63 64 65 66 67 68 69 70 71 72 73 74 75 76 77 78 79 80

10
20
30
40
50
60
70
80
90
100
110
120
130
140
150
160
170
180
190
200
210
220
230
240
250
260
270
280
290
300

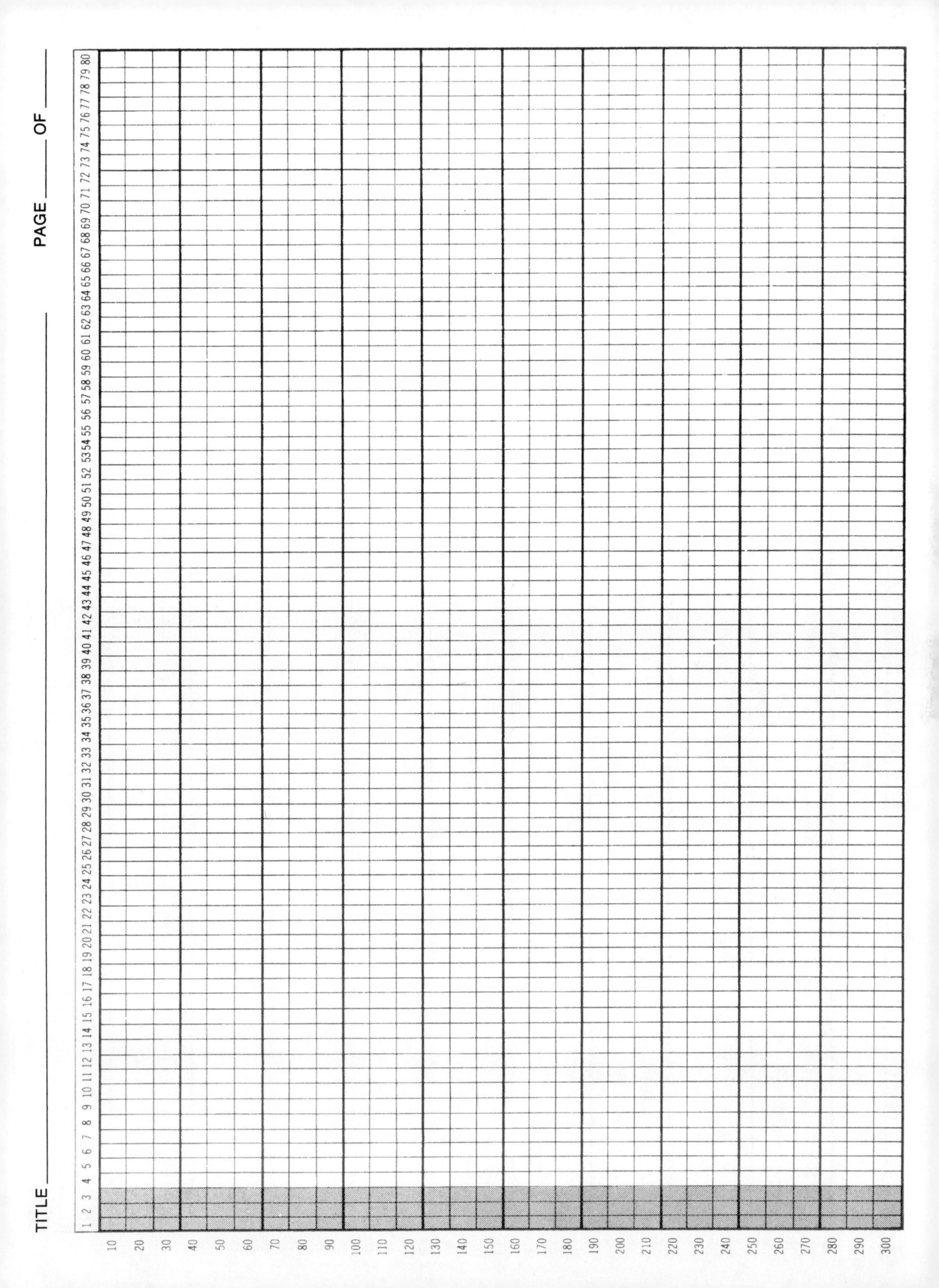

TITLE ______________________________ PAGE ______ OF ______

1 2 3 4 5 6 7 8 9 10 11 12 13 14 15 16 17 18 19 20 21 22 23 24 25 26 27 28 29 30 31 32 33 34 35 36 37 38 39 40 41 42 43 44 45 46 47 48 49 50 51 52 53 54 55 56 57 58 59 60 61 62 63 64 65 66 67 68 69 70 71 72 73 74 75 76 77 78 79 80

10
20
30
40
50
60
70
80
90
100
110
120
130
140
150
160
170
180
190
200
210
220
230
240
250
260
270
280
290
300

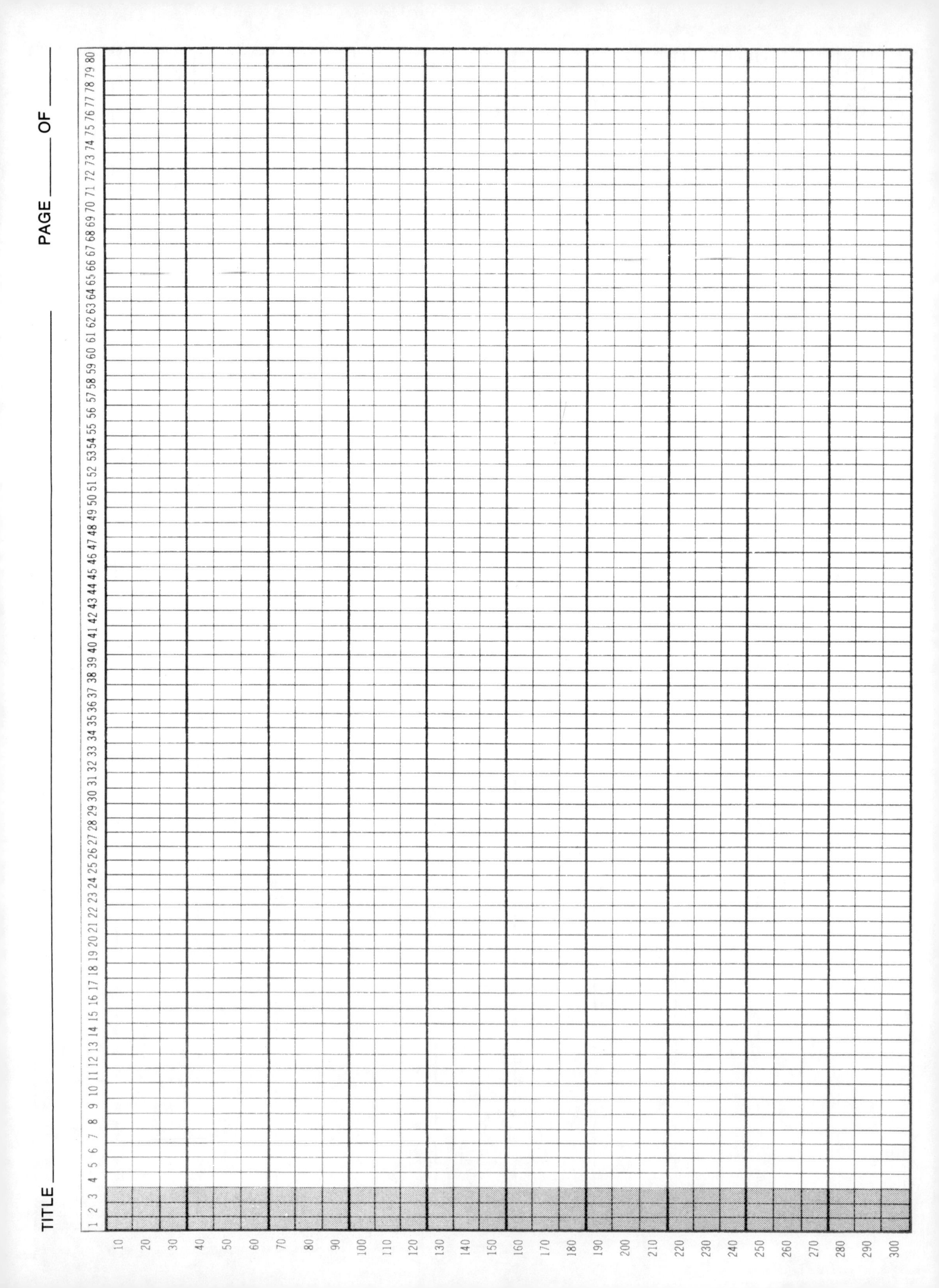

TITLE ______________________________ PAGE ______ OF ______

1 2 3 4 5 6 7 8 9 10 11 12 13 14 15 16 17 18 19 20 21 22 23 24 25 26 27 28 29 30 31 32 33 34 35 36 37 38 39 40 41 42 43 44 45 46 47 48 49 50 51 52 53 54 55 56 57 58 59 60 61 62 63 64 65 66 67 68 69 70 71 72 73 74 75 76 77 78 79 80

10
20
30
40
50
60
70
80
90
100
110
120
130
140
150
160
170
180
190
200
210
220
230
240
250
260
270
280
290
300

TITLE ______________________ PAGE ______ OF ______

1 2 3 4 5 6 7 8 9 10 11 12 13 14 15 16 17 18 19 20 21 22 23 24 25 26 27 28 29 30 31 32 33 34 35 36 37 38 39 40 41 42 43 44 45 46 47 48 49 50 51 52 53 54 55 56 57 58 59 60 61 62 63 64 65 56 67 68 69 70 71 72 73 74 75 76 77 78 79 80

10
20
30
40
50
60
70
80
90
100
110
120
130
140
150
160
170
180
190
200
210
220
230
240
250
260
270
280
290
300

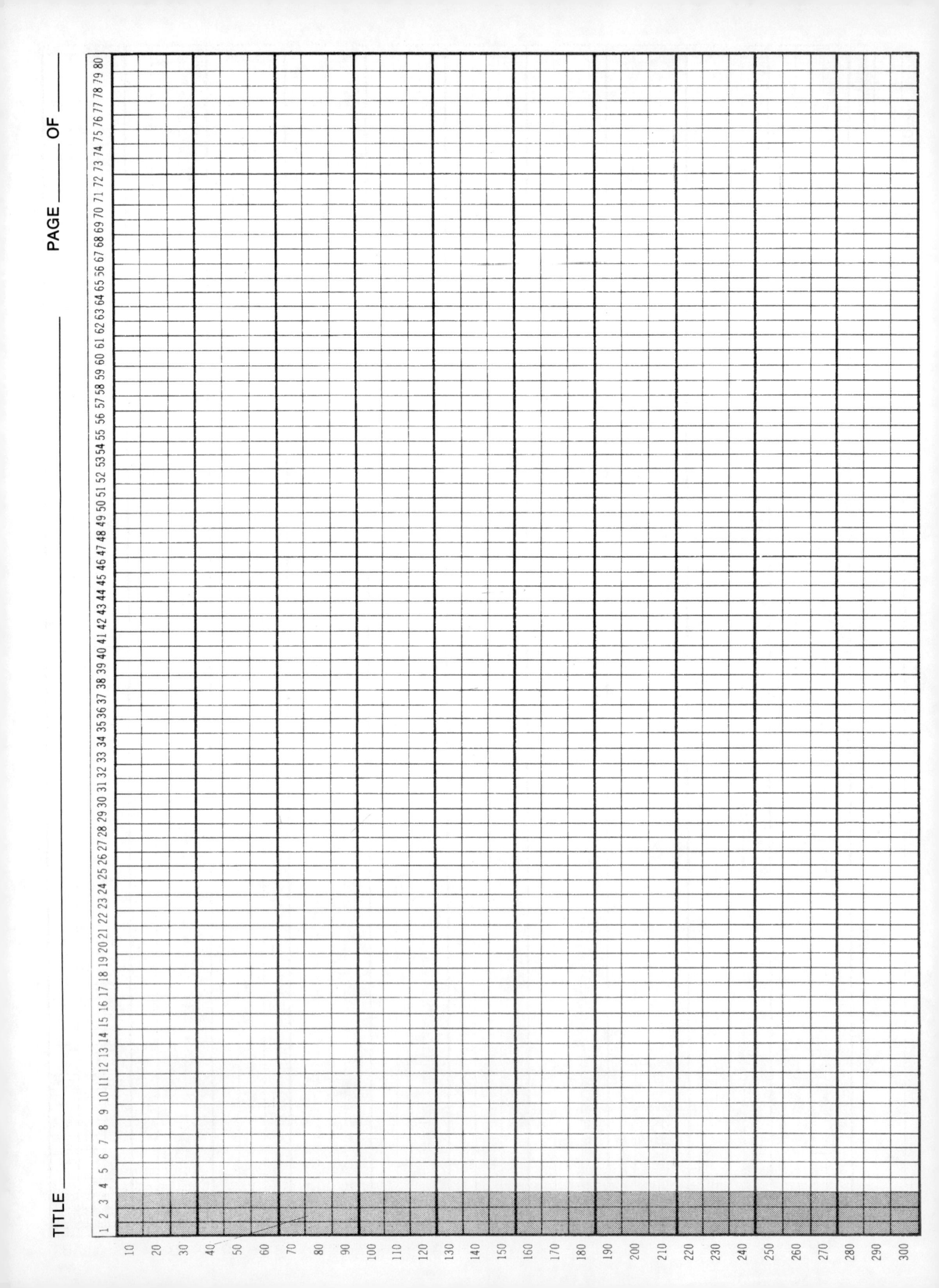

TITLE ______________________________ PAGE ______ OF ______

1 2 3 4 5 6 7 8 9 10 11 12 13 14 15 16 17 18 19 20 21 22 23 24 25 26 27 28 29 30 31 32 33 34 35 36 37 38 39 40 41 42 43 44 45 46 47 48 49 50 51 52 53 54 55 56 57 58 59 60 61 62 63 64 65 66 67 68 69 70 71 72 73 74 75 76 77 78 79 80

10
20
30
40
50
60
70
80
90
100
110
120
130
140
150
160
170
180
190
200
210
220
230
240
250
260
270
280
290
300

TITLE ______________________________ PAGE ______ OF ______

1 2 3 4 5 6 7 8 9 10 11 12 13 14 15 16 17 18 19 20 21 22 23 24 25 26 27 28 29 30 31 32 33 34 35 36 37 38 39 40 41 42 43 44 45 46 47 48 49 50 51 52 53 54 55 56 57 58 59 60 61 62 63 64 65 66 67 68 69 70 71 72 73 74 75 76 77 78 79 80

10
20
30
40
50
60
70
80
90
100
110
120
130
140
150
160
170
180
190
200
210
220
230
240
250
260
270
280
290
300

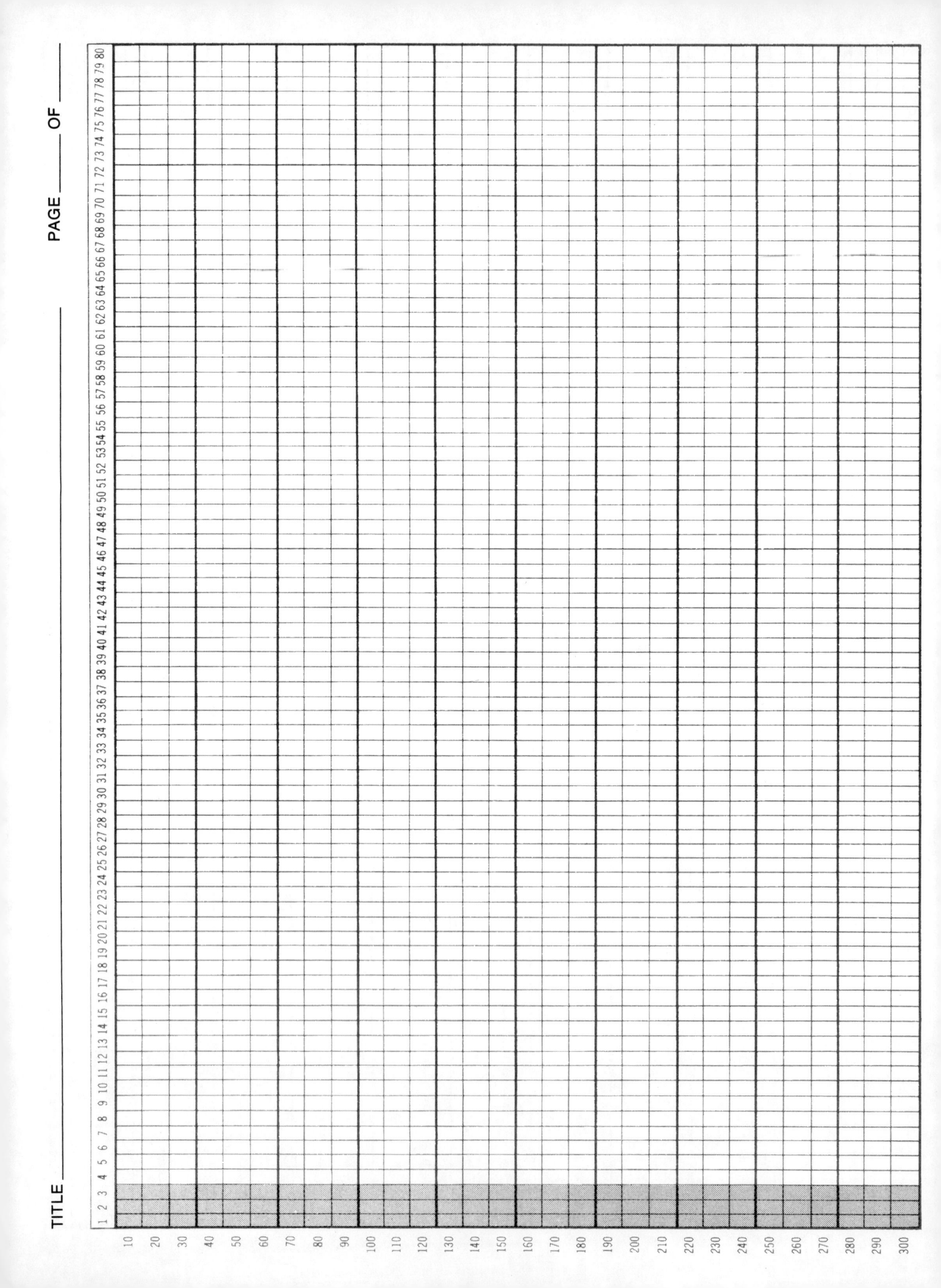

TITLE ______________________________ PAGE ______ OF ______

1 2 3 4 5 6 7 8 9 10 11 12 13 14 15 16 17 18 19 20 21 22 23 24 25 26 27 28 29 30 31 32 33 34 35 36 37 38 39 40 41 42 43 44 45 46 47 48 49 50 51 52 53 54 55 56 57 58 59 60 61 62 63 64 65 66 67 68 69 70 71 72 73 74 75 76 77 78 79 80

10
20
30
40
50
60
70
80
90
100
110
120
130
140
150
160
170
180
190
200
210
220
230
240
250
260
270
280
290
300

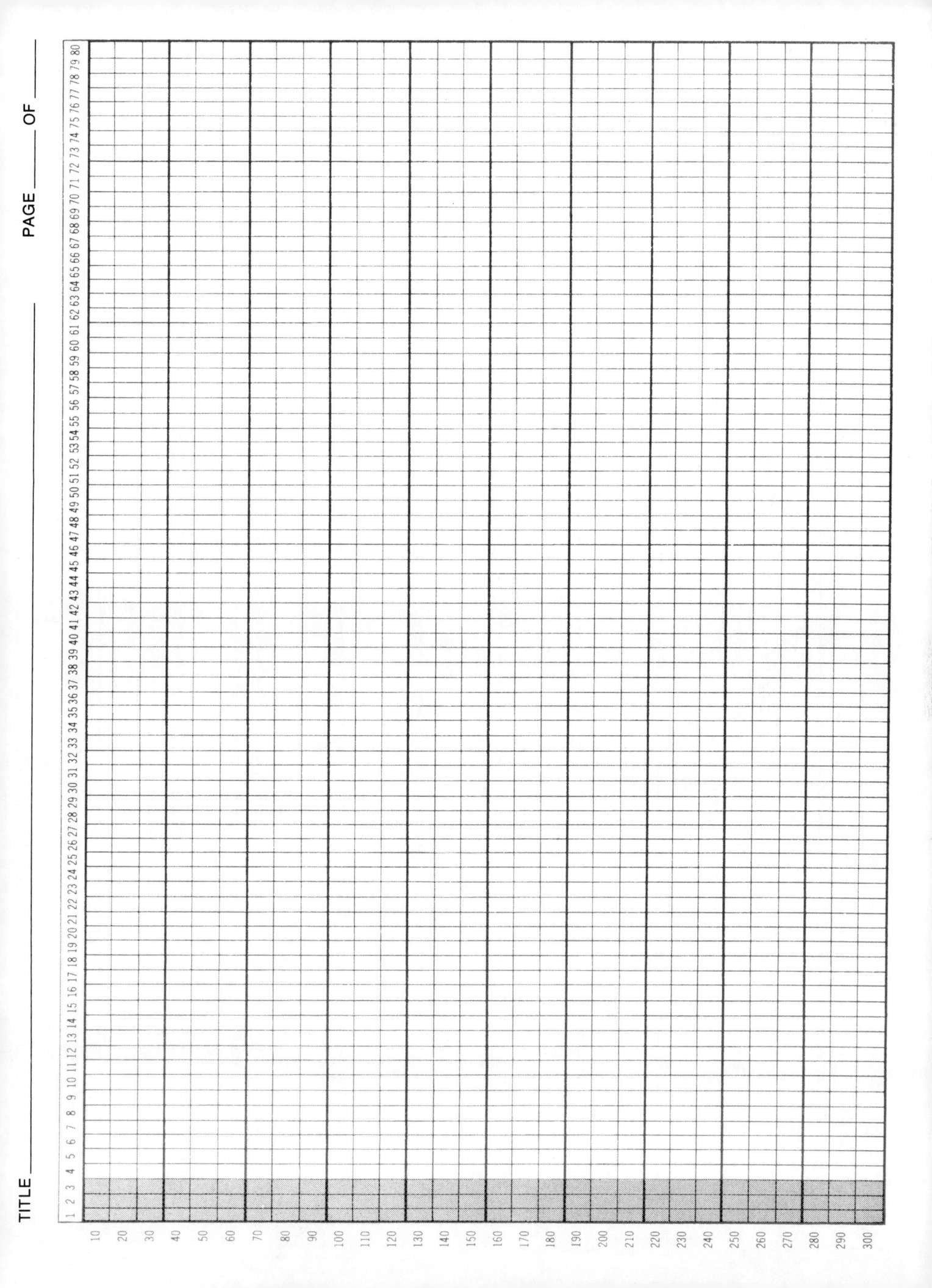

TITLE _____   PAGE ____ OF ____

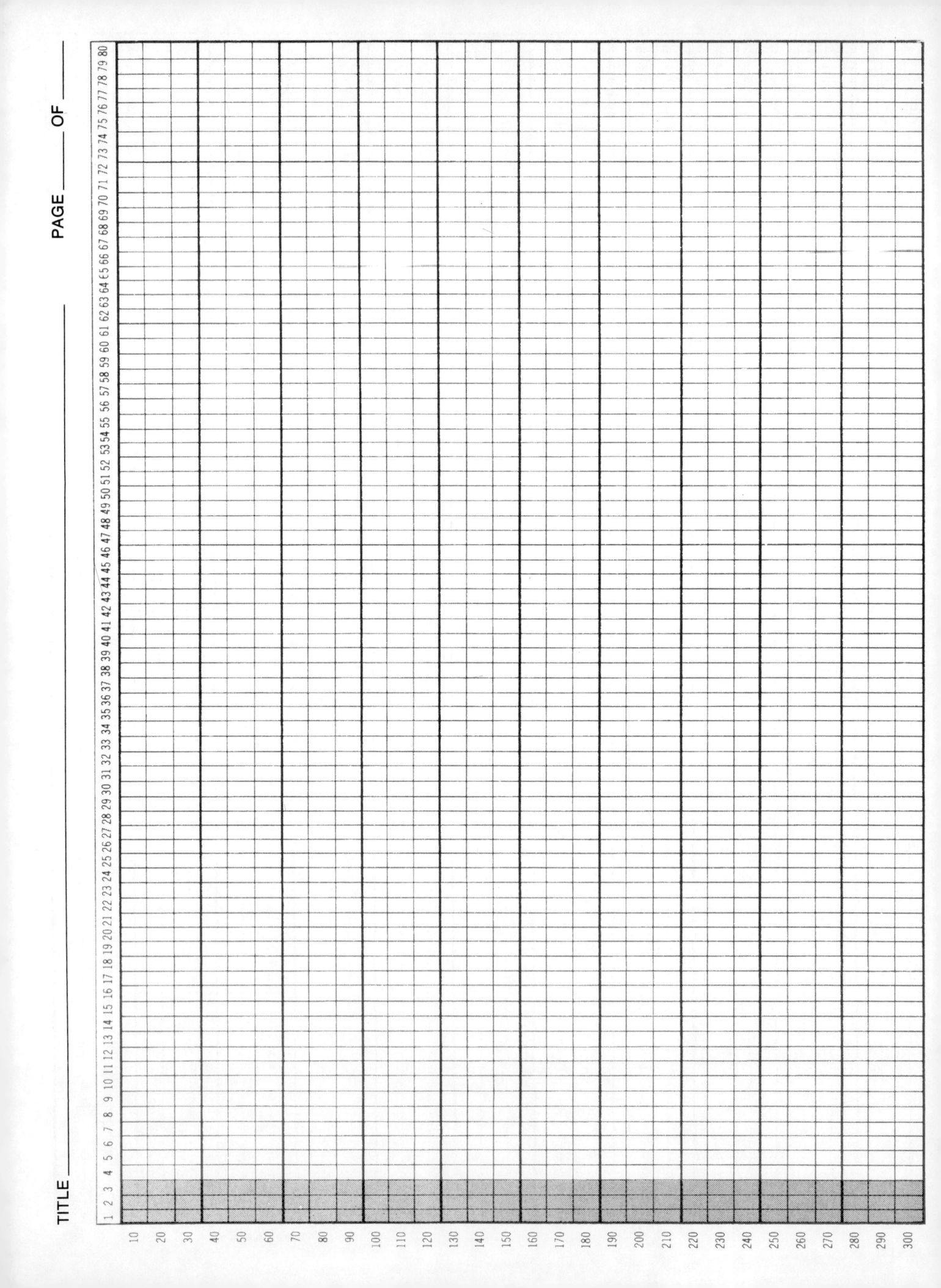

TITLE ________________ PAGE ______ OF ______

1 2 3 4 5 6 7 8 9 10 11 12 13 14 15 16 17 18 19 20 21 22 23 24 25 26 27 28 29 30 31 32 33 34 35 36 37 38 39 40 41 42 43 44 45 46 47 48 49 50 51 52 53 54 55 56 57 58 59 60 61 62 63 64 65 66 67 68 69 70 71 72 73 74 75 76 77 78 79 80

10
20
30
40
50
60
70
80
90
100
110
120
130
140
150
160
170
180
190
200
210
220
230
240
250
260
270
280
290
300

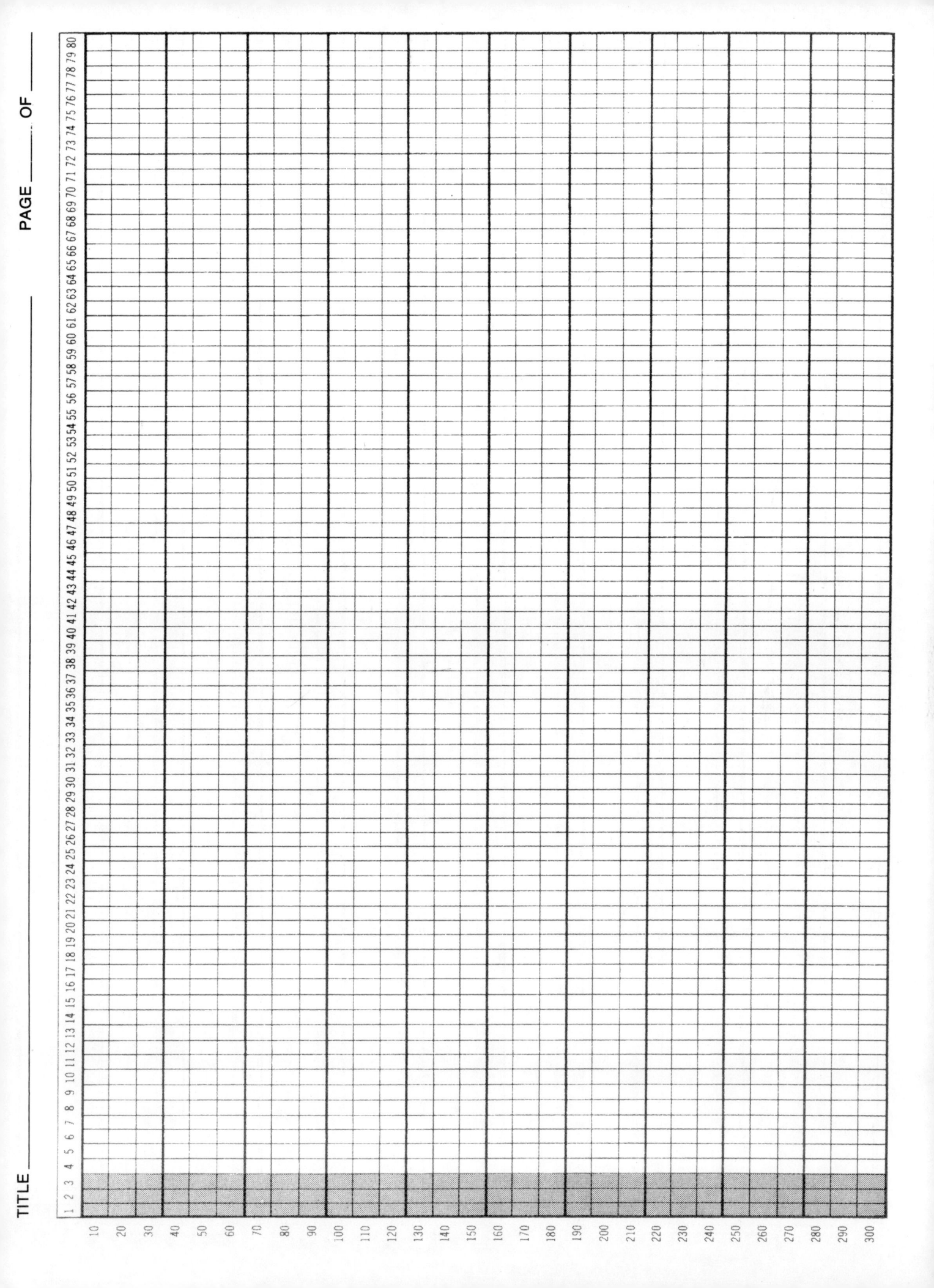

TITLE ______________________ PAGE ______ OF ______

1 2 3 4 5 6 7 8 9 10 11 12 13 14 15 16 17 18 19 20 21 22 23 24 25 26 27 28 29 30 31 32 33 34 35 36 37 38 39 40 41 42 43 44 45 46 47 48 49 50 51 52 53 54 55 56 57 58 59 60 61 62 63 64 65 66 67 68 69 70 71 72 73 74 75 76 77 78 79 80

10
20
30
40
50
60
70
80
90
100
110
120
130
140
150
160
170
180
190
200
210
220
230
240
250
260
270
280
290
300

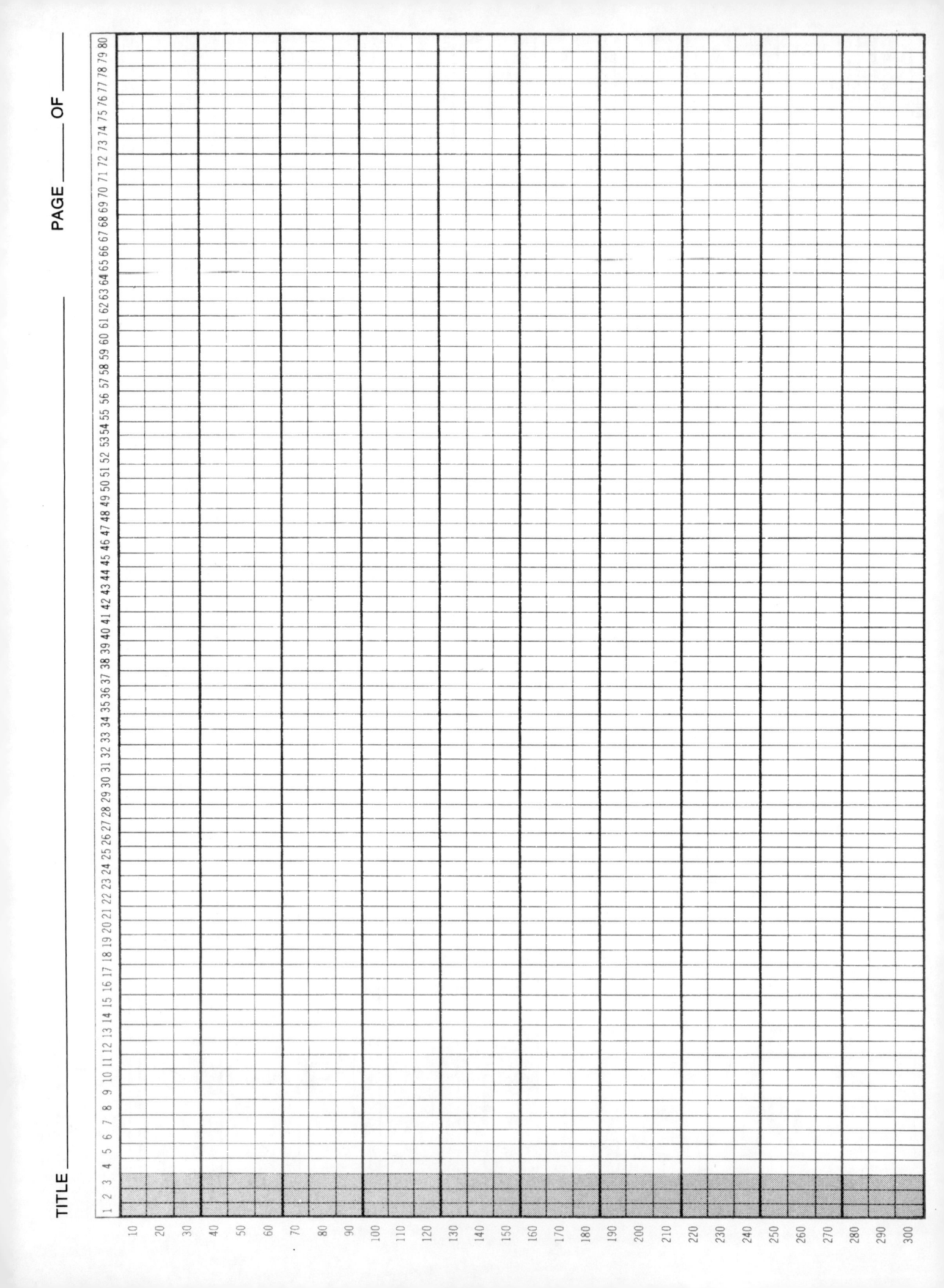

TITLE ______________________________ PAGE ______ OF ______

1 2 3 4 5 6 7 8 9 10 11 12 13 14 15 16 17 18 19 20 21 22 23 24 25 26 27 28 29 30 31 32 33 34 35 36 37 38 39 40 41 42 43 44 45 46 47 48 49 50 51 52 53 54 55 56 57 58 59 60 61 62 63 64 65 66 67 68 69 70 71 72 73 74 75 76 77 78 79 80

10
20
30
40
50
60
70
80
90
100
110
120
130
140
150
160
170
180
190
200
210
220
230
240
250
260
270
280
290
300

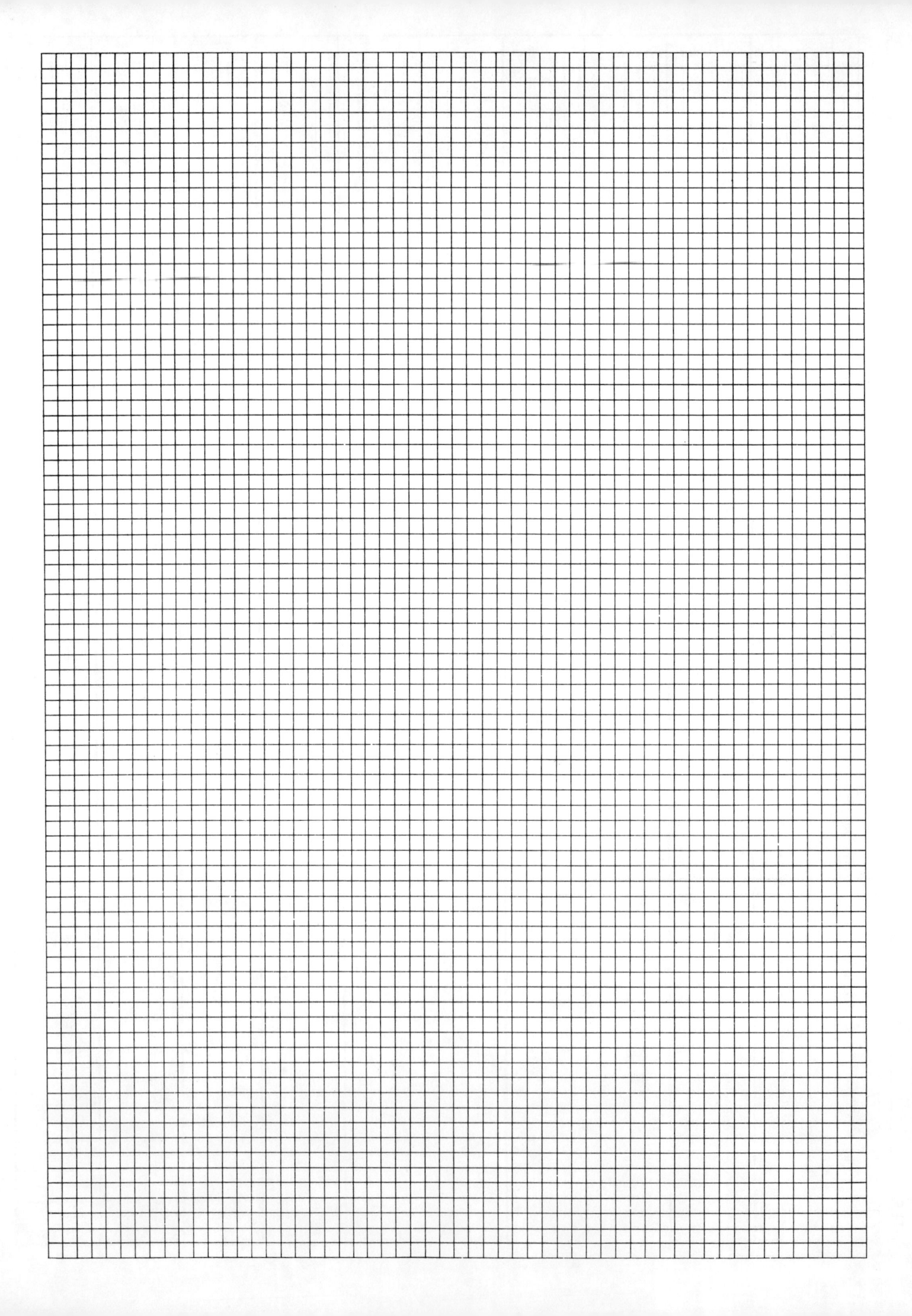

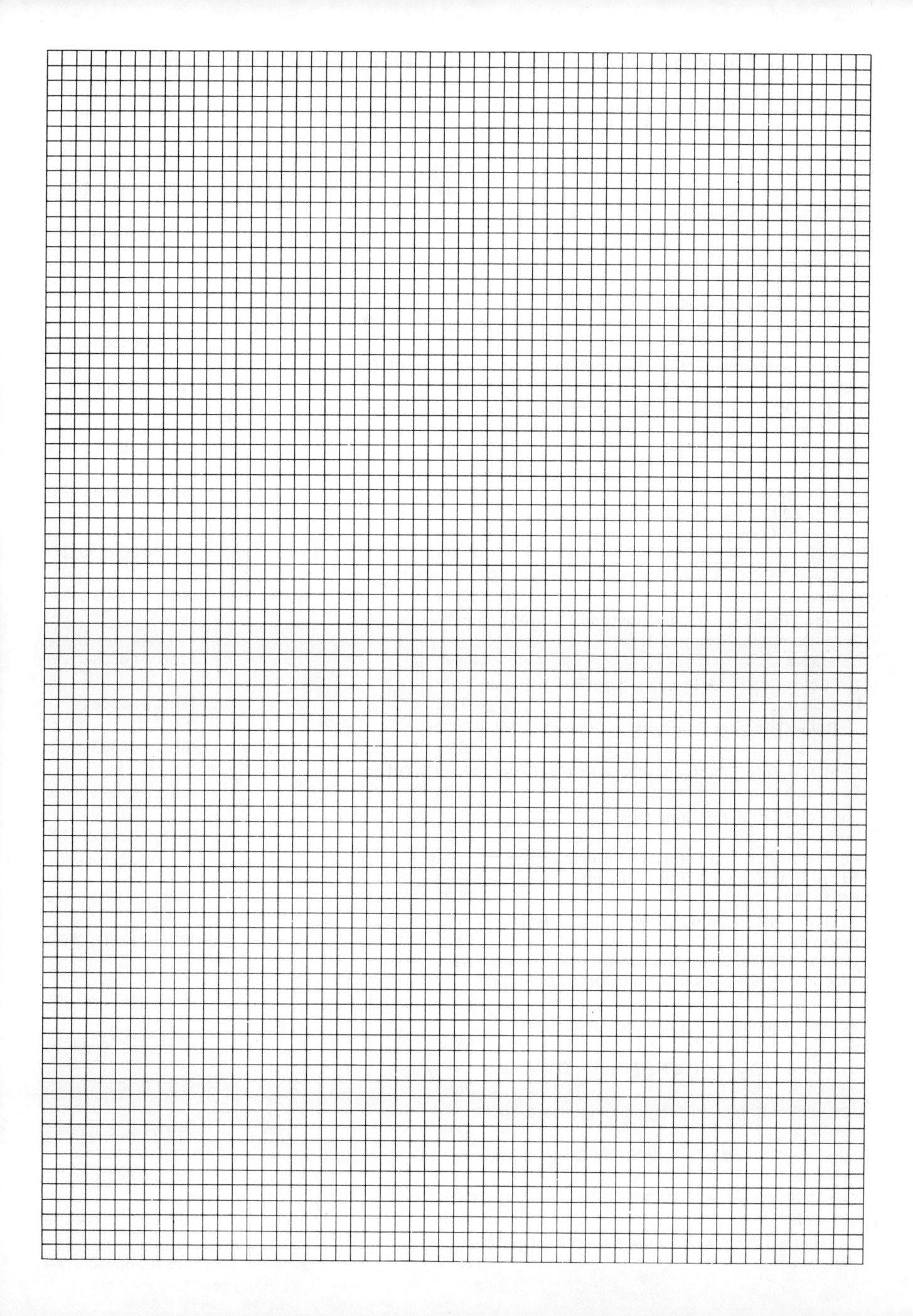

Computer books from ARCsoft Publishers

For the TIMEX/Sinclair 1000, Sinclair ZX-81 and MicroAce:

Practical TIMEX/Sinclair Computer Programs for Beginners
Edward Page — $7.95 — ISBN 0-86668-027-6

101 TIMEX 1000/Sinclair ZX-81 Programming Tips & Tricks
Edward Page — $7.95 — ISBN 0-86668-020-9

TIMEX/Sinclair Computer Games Programs
Edward Page — $7.95 — ISBN 0-86668-026-8

37 TIMEX 1000/Sinclair ZX-81 Programs for Home, School & Office
Edward Page — $8.95 — ISBN 0-86668-021-7

For the Texas Instruments TI-99/4A Home Computer:

101 Programming Tips & Tricks for the Texas Instruments TI-99/4A
Len Turner — $8.95 — ISBN 0-86668-025-X

36 Texas Instruments TI-99/4A Programs for Home, School & Office
Len Turner — $8.95 — ISBN 0-86668-024-1

For the VIC-20 and Commodore computers:

101 Programming Tips & Tricks for the VIC-20
Howard Adler — $8.95 — ISBN 0-86668-030-6

34 VIC-20 Computer Programs for Home, School & Office
Howard Adler — $8.95 — ISBN 0-86668-029-2

For the ATARI 400, 600, 800, 1200XL computers:

101 ATARI Computer Programming Tips & Tricks
Alan North — $8.95 — ISBN 0-86668-022-5

31 New ATARI Computer Programs for Home, School & Office
Alan North — $8.95 — ISBN 0-86668-018-7

For the TRS-80 Color Computer and TDP-100 computers:

Color Computer Graphics
Ron Clark — $9.95 — ISBN 0-86668-012-8

101 Color Computer Programming Tips & Tricks
Ron Clark — $7.95 — ISBN 0-86668-007-1

55 Color Computer Programs for Home School & Office
Ron Clark — $9.95 — ISBN 0-86668-005-5

55 MORE Color Computer Programs for Home, School & Office
Ron Clark — $9.95 — ISBN 0-86668-008-X

The Color Computer Songbook
Ron Clark — $7.95 — ISBN 0-86668-011-X

For the APPLE and Franklin ACE computers:

101 APPLE Computer Programming Tips & Tricks
Fred White — $8.95 — ISBN 0-86668-015-2

33 New APPLE Computer Programs for Home, School & Office
Fred White — $8.95 — ISBN 0-86668-016-0

For the TRS-80, Sharp and Casio Pocket Computers:

Practical PC-2/PC-1500 Pocket Computer Programs
Jim Cole — $7.95 — ISBN 0-86668-028-4

Pocket Computer Programming Made Easy
Jim Cole — $8.95 — ISBN 0-86668-009-8

99 Tips & Tricks for the New Pocket Computers
Jim Cole — $7.95 — ISBN 0-86668-019-5

101 Pocket Computer Programming Tips & Tricks
Jim Cole — $7.95 — ISBN 0-86668-004-7

Murder In The Mansion and Other Computer Adventures—2nd Edition
Jim Cole — $6.95 — ISBN 0-86668-501-4

50 MORE Programs in BASIC for Home, School & Office
Jim Cole — $9.95 — ISBN 0-86668-003-9

35 Practical Programs for the CASIO Pocket Computer
Jim Cole — $8.95 — ISBN 0-86668-014-4